CW00530358

The Random Book of…

JOHN

Well, I didn't know that!

All statistics, facts and figures are correct as of March 31st 2009.

© Stewart Cruttenden
Stewart Cruttenden has asserted his rights in accordance with the
Copyright, Designs and Patents Act 1988 to be identified
as the author of this work.

Published By:

Stripe Publishing Ltd
First Floor, 3 St. Georges Place, Brighton, BN1 4GA

Email: info@stripepublishing.co.uk
Web: www.stripepublishing.co.uk

First published 2009

A catalogue record for this book is available from the British Library.

10-digit ISBN: 1-907158-05-7
13-digit ISBN: 978-1-907158-05-6

Printed and bound by Gutenberg Press Ltd., Malta.

Editor: Dan Tester
Illustrations: Jonathan Pugh (www.pughcartoons.co.uk)
Typesetting: Andrew Searle
Cover: Andy Heath

Thanks to my lovely wife, Karen, for her patience and for making life beautiful in too many ways to mention.

Stewart Cruttenden – March 2009

INTRODUCTION

What's in a name?

When parents choose an exotic moniker for their offspring do they realise their choice may have a serious effect on the child's life and personality?

On the other hand, opting for a strong and classic name such as John is likely to have a positive impact on your youngster. Johns have been responsible for some of the human race's major scientific advancements and artistic accomplishments.

Johns have excelled in the fields of law, military service and politics.

And, in sport, literature, comedy and film.

Wherever you see human triumphs – and, admittedly, disaster – you will find a John in command, at the helm or simply messing things up.

So, whatever our own names, let's try to persuade parents to reconsider naming their boys John instead of Abundie, Beegie, Burritt or Dainis.

We all know that the world would be a better and more sensible place if they did.

Stewart Cruttenden – March 2009

WHAT DOES JOHN MEAN, EXACTLY?

The name John is of Hebrew origin. It derives from יֽוֹחָנָן (Yo-HAN-an), meaning 'God is Gracious' and owes its early popularity to two prominent New Testament personalities. The first, **John the Baptist**, baptised Jesus Christ in the Jordan River.

The second was **Saint John the Evangelist**, the longest lived of the 12 apostles, writer of the fourth Gospel and three epistles, and – although disputed by some – the cataclysmic Book of Revelation.

The name was common among Eastern Christians in the Byzantine Empire and flourished in Western Europe after the First Crusade. It became popular in England, being given to 20 per cent of the country's boys in the late Middle Ages.

John was fashionable until the 20th century but went from being the fifth most-used name in 1964 to languishing outside the top 50 by 1998.

Variants exist in most languages, including: Jan in Dutch and Slavic; Janos, Czech; Joao, Portuguese; and the Johan variations in German.

It's probably the most widely used name in history: kings, popes, saints, heroes, villains, and men of every type have been called John.

Surnames that derive from John include Johnson, Johnston, Johnstone and Johns. John itself is a popular surname.

JOHN IN OTHER COUNTRIES

Eoin	(Irish language derivation of Seán; in Irish and Scottish Gaelic refers to the Apostle)
Evan	(Anglicised form of Welsh Ieuan or Ifan)
Giovanni, **Gianni**	(Italian)
Gjon	(Albania)
Giuàn	(Western Lombard)
Gwanni, **Gwann**, **Ganni**	(Maltese)
Ian	(Scottish derived from Gaelic Iain)
Ioannis, **Giannis**	(Greek)
Ion	(Romanian)
Ivan	(Bulgarian, Croatian, Russian and other Slavic language nations)
Jan	(Norwegian, Dutch, Swedish, Faroese, Polish, Czech, German)
Ján	(Slovak)
Janez	(Slovenian)
Jani	(Finnish)
Janis	(Latvian)
János	(Hungarian)
Jean	(French)
Jens	(Danish, Norwegian, Swedish)
Jevan	(variation of Evan)
Joan	(Catalan)
João	(Portuguese)
Joanes	(Basque)
Jógvan	(Faroese)
Johan	(Dutch, Swedish, Danish, Norwegian, German, Faroese)
Johann	(Germanic: German, Danish, Norwegian, Swedish, Dutch)
Johannes	(Germanic: German, Danish, Norwegian, Swedish, Dutch)
Jon	(Norwegian, Swedish, Basque)
Jón	(Icelandic, Faroese)
Jonas	(Lithuanian, Swedish)
Joni	(Fijian)
Jovan	(Serbian)

Juan	(Spanish/Filipino), feminine form Juana with diminutive Juanita
Juhani	(Finnish)
Seán	(Irish Seán, after the French Jean)
Shane	(anglicised form of Seán)
Shaun	(anglicised form of Seán)
Shawn	(anglicised form of Seán)
Shon	(Israeli Hebrew)
Siôn	(Welsh)
Yohanu	(Telugu)
Yohanes	(Eritrean)
Yohannan	(Malayalam)
Yohani	(Kirundi)

EVERYMAN JOHNS

The 18th century satirist **Dr. John Arbuthnot** invented the rotund **John Bull** as the personification of Great Britain, dressed in white breeches and characterised by commonsense, a love of beer and fierce loyalty to friends.

By the 20th century he was generally drawn wearing a top hat and Union Flag waistcoat, accompanied by a bulldog. He had been disowned by all parts of Britain except England where he is still a recognised figure.

Most English-speaking countries use John or Joe for their 'everyman'. In England, it's Joe Bloggs, and in the USA it's **John Doe**.

It first appeared in 1215 in Britain's *Magna Carta* where the names John Doe and Richard Roe were used to hide witnesses' identities in landlord-tenant disputes.

After appearing in John and Michael Danim's 1825 book, *Tales by the O'Hara Family*, it was an accepted term in the USA and, later, New Zealand. A chilling use of the moniker is in court or hospital morgues for unknown dead men. Some non-English speaking countries have John-like everymen, such as **Jean Dupont** in France and Belgium, and **Juan Perez** in Bolivia.

John Doe, born **John Duchac** in 1954, was founder and bass player for X, the 1980s American punk-rock band. He's also an actor, appearing on hit TV shows such as *Carnivale* and *Roswell*.

A **'Dear John'** is a letter from a woman to break up a romance. The phrase originated in World War II when many wives and girlfriends ditched men who were stationed overseas in favour of one closer to home. Most love letters began with affectionate greetings, such as 'My Darling John' or 'My Dearest John', so an abrupt 'Dear John' would signal the unhappy message.

The phrase inspired a 1960s Swedish film, British and American sitcoms, a 2006 book by Nicholas Sparks and songs by Hank Williams, Elton John, Keith Green, Status Quo, Ilse de Lange, Ryan Adams and the Cardinals.

John Henry is the black hero of a folk ballad in the USA. The song tells of a contest when Henry crushed more rock than a new invention, the steam drill, but died *"with his hammer in his hand"*. He's regarded by romantics as a symbol of working class man's doomed fight against progress and of the black man's battle with the white.

A 1970s racehorse named after him became the biggest money-earner in the history of American thoroughbred racing, winning more than $6.5 million between 1977 and 1984. John Henry lived in happy retirement when he went out to stud at the Kentucky Horse Park.

JOHN SMITHS

John Smith succeeded Neil Kinnock as leader of Britain's opposition Labour Party in 1992. The MP for North Lanarkshire died suddenly of a heart attack two years later, aged 55, at London's St. Bartholomew's Hospital.

He had visited the hospital two weeks earlier to campaign against its closure. He would almost certainly have been a traditional socialist Prime Minister if he'd won the 1997 General Election, and Tony Blair's 'New Labour' would never have come to power.

Captain John Smith was a 17th century English sailor, soldier and writer and a leader of the group that colonised Virginia (now an American state) for the profit of the Virginia Company of London. Among his many claims was that Native American girl Pocahontas twice saved his life.

He was a major character in the Disney animation *Pocahontas*, where he was voiced by Mel Gibson. Colin Farrell played him in the film *The New World*.

John Smith started brewing ale in Tadcaster, Yorkshire, in 1847. He died in 1879 but the family brewery he founded still produces John Smith's 'No Nonsense Beers', most recently advertised by comedian Peter Kay.

John Smith's is Britain's most popular bitter, selling more than a million pints a day.

Deaf comedian **John Smith** joined the stand-up comedy circuit in 2005 and his act – performed in British Sign Language (BSL) – remains popular all over the country. In a reverse of the usual way of things, his set is translated from BSL into English and is enjoyed by deaf and non-deaf audiences.

Sir John Smith CBE and OBE was a director of toffs' bank Coutts & Co. for more than 40 years and Conservative MP for the Cities of London and Westminster for five years.

After a lifetime of achievement he's best remembered for founding the Landmark Trust, the charity that preserved and refurbished more than 200 British buildings of character and heritage.

⟫◆⟪

REAL JOHNS

Ozzy Osbourne, self-styled 'Godfather of Heavy Metal' was born John Michael Osbourne in 1948. He was vocalist of Black Sabbath, made famous – or infamous – in the 1970s by their hit single Paranoid and by Ozzy's biting off a dove's head during a publicity stunt. In 1982, he bit the head off a bat on stage, claiming he thought it was made of rubber.

He revelled in the nickname 'Prince of Darkness' and was accused of Satanism by religious groups. Two sets of

American parents sued him but failed to convince the courts that his lyrics had led to their children's suicides.

Despite well-documented problems with alcohol and drugs, Ozzy won several platinum records and earned a fortune of more than £50 million. He achieved unlikely global celebrity status with the MTV reality show *The Osbournes*.

English punk rockers the Sex Pistols, led by vocalist **Johnny Rotten** (b. John Lydon 1956) and bass guitarist Sid Vicious (b. John Ritchie 1957), lasted just three years from 1975 with four singles and one album, but enjoyed notoriety generated by foul language on TV, anarchic lyrics and huge brawls at their gigs.

Lydon's colourful life was nearly extinguished in December 1988 when a row with his wife over her late holiday packing led to their cancelling reservations on Pan Am Flight 103 which blew up over Lockerbie, Scotland, in a terrorist attack.

Vicious, named after Rotten's hamster which bit the bassist on the finger, was so terrible at playing that he was replaced by stand-ins on record and his amplifier was turned off at concerts.

Vicious' final days saw him charged with the fatal stabbing of his girlfriend Nancy Spungen in a New York hotel before he died of a heroin overdose, aged just 21.

Joe Strummer, born John Mellor in 1952, the leader of
legendary band The Clash, wrote original music for the film
Sid and Nancy, based on the lives of the Sex Pistol.

The band's biggest hits included London Calling and White
Man in Hammersmith Palais, while Should I Stay Or
Should I Go became their first USA hit.

Rolling Stone magazine named their album London Calling
as the best of the 1980s.

After briefly deputising for Shane MacGowan as lead singer
with The Pogues, he resisted invitations to re-form The Clash,
reportedly turning down a £3 million offer to tour the USA.

"That was never The Clash way of doing things," he told *The
Times*. "We all agreed it would have been sickening to have
been playing that music with the pound signs hanging over us."

John Ronald Reuel Tolkien, better known by his initials
J. R. R. Tolkien, achieved worldwide fame and fortune
for his fantasy novel *The Lord of the Rings*, written between
1927 and 1939 and published in 1954. The huge tome
won a new audience with Peter Jackson's movie trilogy, and
in 2008, *The Times* placed him sixth on a list of 'The 50
greatest British writers since 1945'.

The world nearly missed the legendary work as Tolkien saw
action in World War I's Battle of the Somme. Many of his
close friends were killed and he was invalided out of the
army with trench fever.

John le Carré, born David Cornwell in 1931, began writing espionage novels in the 1960s while working for MI6. His cover as a secret agent was blown by British double agent Kim Philby who inspired the character of Gerald, the mole hunted by George Smiley in le Carré's bestseller, *Tinker, Tailor, Soldier, Spy*.

John Wayne was christened with the un-macho name of Marion Robert Morrison. He started his career as a £40 a week stuntman and went on to play the leading role in 142 of his 175 films, mainly Westerns and war movies.

He achieved just one Best Actor Oscar, for *True Grit* in 1969. A year earlier he directed *The Green Berets*, the only movie made during the Vietnam War which was pro-conflict and one of only two films directed by Wayne.

Charlton Heston, born John Carter in 1923, had a commanding 6ft 3ins. physique, square jaw and looks that made him the archetypal all-American, movie action hero. He missed out on an Oscar in 1953 when studio bosses overruled director Billy Wilder's wish to cast Heston in *Stalag 17*.

William Holden was voted Best Actor instead. Six years later, Heston won the coveted gong with the title role in *Ben-Hur*, after Marlon Brando, Burt Lancaster and Rock Hudson had turned down the part.

An anti-racist Democrat supporter in the 1960s, Heston became an ultra right wing campaigner for Republican presidents, chairman of the pro-gun pressure group the National Rifle Association and vocal supporter of American wars.

Few people are famous for a single sentence but that's what happened to a boy born into poverty in Wales as John Rowlands, in 1941, before emigrating to New Orleans, Louisiana, aged 15.

He took the name **Henry Morton Stanley** and as a journalist for the *New York Herald* was assigned to Africa to find missing explorer David Livingstone.

After months of trekking through dense jungle, Stanley found his man in November 1981, and famously enquired: "Dr. Livingstone, I presume?" an understatement thought to be quintessentially British.

Born John Lemmon in 1925, Harvard Business School graduate **Jack Lemmon** shocked his father by working as a pianist in a New York City dive. He was later plucked from TV serials and sitcoms to become a Hollywood superstar where he was the first actor to win an Oscar for lead and supporting roles: as supporting actor in *Mister Roberts* (1955) and the star of *Save the Tiger* (1973), a movie he helped to fund by working for just £90 a week.

He appeared in ten movies in 40 years with his friend Walter Matthau – and both men insisted they never had a single argument.

Dizzy Gillespie, one of jazz's most influential musicians was born John Birks Gillespie, the youngest of nine children in South Carolina in 1917. He began to play the piano at four and became a celebrated trumpeter, singer, band leader and composer.

Mystery surrounds his famous 'bent trumpet' that gave him a unique sound and helped to make him a legend. He said it was due to accidental damage during a 1953 gig, but his biographer, Alyn Shipton, claimed Gillespie stole the idea when he saw one in 1937 while on tour in England.

Movie legend and hell-raiser **Jack Nicholson** was born John Joseph Nicholson in 1937. He has won three Oscars, a record for male actors he shares with Walter Brennan. His first Hollywood job was as a runner for the Hanna-Barbera animation company who offered Jack, a gifted artist, a full-time animator position.

His big break came when he wrote the screenplay for *The Trip* starring Peter Fonda and Dennis Hopper. The two stars involved him in their next project, *Easy Rider*, as hard-drinking banker George Hanson. Jack later learned his part had been written for Rip Torn who was thrown off the set after a fight with Hopper.

John Michael Crichton, writing under the name Michael, completed his first best-selling novel, *The Andromeda Strain*, in 1969, as a student at Harvard Medical School. He wrote a further 14 novels including *Congo*, *Sphere* and the dinosaur-DNA classics *Jurassic Park* and *Lost World: Jurassic Park II*, and five non-fiction books.

He wrote original screenplays for *Westworld* and *Twister* and was director, producer or writer of a further 11 films. Crichton won an Emmy and a Writers Guild of America Award for his hit TV medical drama series, *ER*.

Of his many awards, Crichton treasured most the naming of an *Ankylosaur Crichtonsaurus bohlini*, a boney herbivorous dinosaur of the Jurassic period, in 2002.

He died in 2008.

⋙◆⋘

WHAT DOES JOHNNY MEAN, EXACTLY?

Johnny Come Lately is a newcomer on the scene, usually with the implication that because he has just shown up, his opinion is likely to be invalid or his advice of little use.

MUSICAL JOHNS

From his birth in Liverpool in1940, during a German
air raid, to his death by the gun of obsessed fan David
Chapman in New York in 1980, **John Lennon** lived an
extraordinary life as a musical icon. His aunt Mimi raised
him, warning: "You'll never make a living out of the
guitar."

In 1957, he met a young man called Paul McCartney and
the rest, as they say, is history. The first Beatles concert
was at the Cavern club in Liverpool on March 21st 1961.
The band became the most popular of all time, selling
more than a billion records. In the UK, more than 40
different Beatles singles, LPs, and EPs reached number one,
including 15 chart-topping albums.

After The Beatles' split in 1969, Lennon pursued a
successful solo career, often featuring second wife Yoko
Ono. American president Richard Nixon tried to deport
him after his song Give Peace a Chance became an anthem
for the anti-Vietnam war movement. But popular support
helped him gain a green card in 1976.

Songwriter and musician **Julian Lennon** was born John
Charles Julian Lennon in 1963, just before his father
became a phenomenon. He was the only child of Lennon's
first wife Cynthia. His birth was concealed as The Beatles'
manager Brian Epstein felt teenage girl fans would be less
enthusiastic about the group if they knew Lennon was a
family man.

Paul McCartney wrote one of the band's biggest hits to console him after of his parents' divorce. Hey Jude was originally Hey Jules, but McCartney changed the name as he thought 'Jude' was easier to sing. Julian was behind the title of one of his dad's songs, Lucy In The Sky With Diamonds, with lyrics describing a picture Julian drew of a classmate named Lucy, surrounded by stars.

John Cummings (b. 1948) and pals Douglas 'Dee Dee' Colvin, a heroin addict and male prostitute, and Jeffrey 'Joey' Hyman, a former mental hospital patient, seemed to have a friendship based on alcohol and solvent abuse. But things changed in 1974 when Cummings bought a guitar and they formed The Ramones, with drummer Tommy Erdelyi.

Cummings changed his name to **Johnny Ramone** after mistakenly adopting Paul McCartney's original stage name, Ramon. The band belted out two or three-minute songs in live sets that lasted less than 20 minutes, and their 1976 debut album, Ramones, featured 14 tracks in less than half an hour.

A *New York Times* poll voted that record one of the 20 most influential of the 20th century, alongside works by Miles Davis, Billie Holiday and Elvis Presley. The group were more successful in the UK where singles included the top ten hit Baby I Love You. Johnny Ramone died of cancer aged 55.

John Mellencamp was born with spina bifida in Indiana in 1951. He was often in trouble with the law as a teenager and formed his first band aged 14. He eloped with his pregnant 17-year-old girlfriend, Pricilla Esterline, and seemed destined for a life of mediocrity.

Aged 24, he went to New York and won a recording deal but fell out with the record company over a covers album called Chestnut Street Incident. He was furious to have been named 'Johnny Cougar' and the record bombed. Two years later his second album, Johnny Cougar, with a different company, included two top 30 singles.

His breakthrough came in 1982 when American Fool soared to number one thanks to the number two hit Hurts So Good and the number one single Jack & Diane, both supported by videos on the new TV station MTV.

The success of American Fool meant he could add 'Mellencamp' to his stage name, and 1983's Uh-Huh was the first album credited to John Cougar Mellencamp.

Jon Bon Jovi was born John Francis Bongiovi Jr. in New Jersey in 1962, and was convinced from his early teens that he would be a rock star. He was playing in clubs at 16 and recorded his first single, Runaway, aged 18.

John started a band signed by PolyGram three years later. The record company anglicised John Bongiovi's name and their self-titled debut came out in January 1984. The album of power ballads went gold and the follow-up, 7800

Farenheit, in April 1985 was popular with fans but hated by critics.

The group silenced all doubters with a third album, Slippery When Wet, which went platinum within six weeks, selling more than 14 million copies. After retiring in 1989, the band re-formed in 1999 with a Grammy-nominated album, Crush, and then, Bounce, in 2002.

Bass guitarist **John Entwistle** joined The Detours, a band that included Roger Daltrey, in 1962. When Pete Townshend, Entwistles's former school friend, and drummer Keith Moon joined, the band changed its name to The Who. They enjoyed chart success in the UK and USA with songs such as My Generation.

John was a talented writer, creating many of the band's numbers, including Boris The Spider, Whiskey Man, Cousin Kevin, and My Wife. The Who were due for a comeback tour in 2002 but Entwistle died in a Las Vegas hotel room from a heart attack brought on by cocaine use.

John Baldry, nicknamed **Long John Baldry** from his height of 6ft 7ins. started as a teenager playing folk and blues in tiny clubs across the UK. A 'nearly man' as far as his own success was concerned, Baldry spurred the careers of several rock greats.

In the 1960s he helped to form Alexis Korner's Blues Incorporated, whose members included future Rolling

Stones Mick Jagger and Charlie Watts. Baldry's own band, the Hoochie Coochie Men, featured Rod Stewart, then an unknown vocalist. A later Baldry creation, Bluesology, had a talented young keyboard player and singer named Reg Dwight, later known as Elton John.

Before fading into oblivion, Baldry enjoyed surprising success with orchestral ballads, including Let The Heartaches Begin, which won a gold record. Friends reckon he could have been one of music's biggest stars if he had not hated publicity and celebrity so much, nor suffered from poor health and phobias. Whenever possible he took the bus as he was terrified of flying.

Johnny Cash was baptised J. R. Cash after his 1932 birth in Arkansas because parents Ray and Carrie couldn't agree on a name. The US Air Force wouldn't accept initials so he called himself John R. Cash when he enlisted, changing his name to Johnny in 1955 with his first recording contract at Sun Records.

In 1957, I Walk The Line was his first number one country hit. Cash moved to California the following year and almost died of addiction to amphetamines and alcohol. Despite his illness, he continued popular success with Ring Of Fire and Understand Your Man.

His second wife, June Carter, helped him kick his drug habit and become a devout Christian fundamentalist. He won two Grammy Awards and wrote the hit singles A Thing Called Love and One Piece At A Time. He died in 2003, four months after the death of the wife who had saved his life.

John Cage (b. 1912) was an American avant-garde composer whose highly unorthodox works have divided critical opinion. Cage believed any sound could constitute music and his most controversial work, 433, comprised four minutes and 33 seconds of 'silence'. 433 features a performer or performers standing on stage but playing no instrument – while the audience listens to the ambient sounds of the concert hall.

Even more bizarre is the piece, As Slow As Possible, whose performance began "with a long pause" in Halberstadt, Germany, in 2001. Organ pedals are held and released by machines and the first chord was played from February 5th 2003 until July 5th 2005. The sixth chord change happened in July 2008 and the work is due to finish in 2640.

John Coltrane, born in 1926 in North Carolina, became an iconic jazz figure during his career as saxophonist, bandleader and composer. Miles Davis kicked him out of his quintet in 1957 because of his alcohol and heroin addictions but took him back from 1958 to 1960.

Coltrane developed his "sheets of sound" approach to improvisation on the tenor sax and his first great recording came in 1957 with Blue Train. He later took up the soprano sax and released highly acclaimed albums Giant Steps, My Favorite Things and A Love Supreme.

His final works Ascension and Meditations in 1965 drew
on his exploration of Islam, Hinduism, the Kabbala, Jiddu
Krishnamurti and astrology. He died from liver cancer, aged
40.

Millions of people have enjoyed **John Williams**' music
without even knowing who he is. He has created music for
some of Hollywood's most celebrated films, including the *Star
Wars* series, *E.T. the Extra Terrestrial*, *Close Encounters of the Third
Kind*, *Jaws*, *Jurassic Park*, and *Schindler's List*.

He has written music for more than 75 films, winning five
Oscars, four Golden Globes, two Emmy Awards, seven
BAFTAs, 20 Grammies and induction into the American
Classical Music Hall of Fame and the Hollywood Bowl Hall
of Fame.

His 45 Oscar nominations make him the second most
nominated person in history (tied with film composer Alfred
Newman) and second only to Walt Disney's 59.

Pop singer-songwriter **John Mayer** won the 2003 Grammy
for Best Male Pop Vocal Performance for the 2002 release of
the single *Your Body Is a Wonderland*. He won that award again
and the Grammy for Song of the Year in 2005 with *Daughters*
from the album *Heavier Things*, beating strong competition
from Elvis Costello, Josh Groban, Prince and Seal.

His on-off romance with former *Friends* actress Jennifer
Aniston has kept gossip columnists busy in recent years.

Bass guitarist **John Deacon** (b. 1951) was the youngest and last of the four members to join Queen and wrote some of their biggest hits, including *You're My Best Friend, Another One Bites the Dust* and *I Want to Break Free*. He also played rhythm and acoustic guitars on several albums as well as occasional keyboards, synthesizer and programming.

Deacon retired from music in the late 1990s, deciding not to participate in the Queen + Paul Rodgers collaboration. He was also absent from Queen's induction into the Rock & Roll Hall of Fame in 2001.

John Barry OBE (b. 1933) won five Oscars and a host of other awards but is best known for his music on 11 James Bond movies. Englishman Barry, real name John Prendergast, received Best Music Score Oscars for *Dances with Wolves* (1990), *Out of Africa* (1985) and *The Lion in Winter* (1968). He won the same award and, with lyricist Don Black, the Best Original Song Oscar for *Born Free* (1966). He won a Golden Globe for *Out of Africa* and an Emmy for *Dances with Wolves*.

The James Bond Theme, one of the most popular pieces of film music, first appeared in *Dr. No* and was originally written by Monty Norman but heavily rearranged by Barry. Lionel Bart was due to do the next Bond score in *From Russia with Love*.

But when Bart revealed he could not read or write music, Barry had his big break to become one of the most successful film music writers of all time.

Singer, songwriter, and guitarist **John Fogerty** (b. 1945) was co-founder, with brother Tom, of Creedence Clearwater Revival. The band's eponymous first album was released in 1968, featuring hit single Suzy Q.

Tom left the band in 1971, and the two other members, bassist Stu Cook and drummer Doug Clifford wanted more of a say in the group's music. John encouraged them to share writing and vocals on the 1972 album, Mardi Gras, but refused to sing any of their songs. The album had poor reviews and sales, prompting them to disband.

Their only reunion with all four original members was at Tom's wedding in 1980.

Stage name	Real name
Michael Stipe (REM)	John Michael Stipe
Fabolous	John Jackson
Fantastic Johnny C.	Johnny Corley
J-Swift	John Martinez
J. Geils	John W. Geils Jr.
J. Valentine	Johnnie Newt
Joe Cocker	John Robert Cocker
John Fred	John Fred Gourrier
John Kay	Joachim Krauledat
John Legend	John Stephens
Johnny Ace	John Alexander
Johnny Mathis	John Royce Mathis
Johnny Paycheck	Don Lytle
Johnny Preston	John Preston Courville

Johnny Rivers   John Ramistella
Murda Mook   John Ancrum
Ras Kass   John Austin

What does John mean, exactly?

John is the slang term for a prostitute's male client. When John was a popular name, most men buying sex would have used it to maintain their privacy.

SONGS WITH JOHN IN THE TITLE

(Big) John Wayne Socks Psychology On The Jaw
– Hatfield and the North
Abraham, Martin & John
– Dion, Harry Belafonte, Smokey Robinson
Ballad Of John and Yoko – The Beatles
Big, Bad John – Jimmy Dean
Dear John – Cyndi Lauper
Dear John – Hank Williams
Dear John – Ryan Adams
Dear John – Status Quo
Dear John Letter
– Jean Shepard, Bobby Bare, Skeeter Davis
Farmer John – The Premiers
From Arik To John – Grace Gale
Geraldine and John – Joe Jackson
Get Up John – Emmylou Harris
God John – The Cassandra Complex
Gris John – Dr John
I Just Shot John Lennon – The Cranberries
I Love John, She Loves Paul – Beulah
Jilted John – Jilted John
John Barbour – Great Big Sea
John Brown – Bob Dylan
John Deere Green – Joe Diffie
John Finn's Wife – Nick Cave and the Bad Seeds
John Gets Leftovers Again – A Minor Forest
John Haber – Bill Morrissey
John Hardy Was a Desperate Little Man
– The Carter Family
John Henry – Harry Belafonte

John Henry – Woody Guthrie
John I Love You – Sinead O'Connor
John Kanaka – Don Sineti and Chris Morgan
John Kettley Is A Weatherman – A Tribe of Toffs
John Lee Supertaster – They Might Be Giants
John O'Dreams – Garnet Rogers
John Prine – Low
John Sinclair – John Lennon
John Smith – Graham Kendrick
John The 23rd – Sarah Slean
John The Baptist – John Martyn
John The Fisherman – Primus
John The Revelator – Depeche Mode
John The Revelator
– Harry Belafonte, The White Stripes
John Walker's Blues – Steve Earle
John Wayne Gacy, Jr. – Sufjan Stevens
John Wayne Is Big Leggy – Haysi Fantayzee
John's Abbey – Keith Jarrett
John, I'm Only Dancing – David Bowie
Letter To A John – Ani DiFranco
Lost John – Lonnie Donegan
Mad John – The Small Faces
My Little John Henry – Alan Lomax
No Bed For Beatle John – Yoko Ono
No Xmas For John Quays – The Fall
Not Now John – Pink Floyd
Put Your Dukes Up, John
– The Little Flames, Arctic Monkeys
Regular John – Queens of the Stone Age
Sleepy-Eyed John – Johnny Horton
Sloop John B. – Beach Boys

Song For John Davis – The Mountain Goats
The Story Of John Henry's Hammer – Johnny Cash
This Time, John – Stina Nordenstam
Ullo John! Gotta New Motor? – Alexei Sayle
Uncle John's Band – The Grateful Dead
Who Killed John Columbo? – Wesley Willis

◄─►◄─►

UK PLACES WITH JOHN IN THE TITLE

Most people presume **John o' Groats** in Caithness,
Scotland, to be the most northern point of the British
mainland but Dunnet Head to the west extends further
north, and Duncansby Head to the east is almost two miles
more distant from Land's End in Cornwall. The sign above
the harbour at John o' Groats says it's 874 miles from
Land's End and for some reason, John o' Groats is the place
people start or finish if they want to cover the length of
Britain.

The record time for a runner to complete the route, as
reported by the Land's End John O'Groats Club, is nine
days and two hours, by Andi Rivett. The aptly named Ben
Stiff holds the skateboarding record as the fastest, in 28
days, and youngest, aged 18.

Andy Wilkinson holds the cycling record, in 41 hours,
four minutes and 22 seconds on a recumbent tricycle. The
record for a conventional bike is 44 hours, four minutes and
20 seconds, by Gethin Butler in 2001.

Richard Elloway of Somerset claims to be the first person to complete the route in both directions for free by local buses, taking two weeks, eight hours and 30 minutes.

Aldbrough St. John	Yorkshire
Barford St. John	Oxfordshire
Berwick St. John	Wiltshire
Cranford St. John	Northamptonshire
Don Johns	Essex
Holbeach St. John	Lincolnshire
John O'Gaunt	Leicestershire
John O'Gaunts	Yorkshire
Johnby	Cumberland
John's Cross	Sussex
John's Hill	Norfolk
John's Town	Carmarthenshire
Johnshaven	Kincardineshire
Johnson Fold	Lancashire
Johnson Street	Norfolk
Johnson's Hillock	Lancashire
Johnston	Lanarkshire
Johnston	Pembrokeshire
Johnston	North Pembrokeshire
Johnstone	Renfrewshire
Johnstone	Dumfriesshire
Johnstonebridge	Dumfriesshire
Johnstounburn	East Lothian
Johnstown	Denbighshire
Johnstown	Carmarthenshire
Long John's Hill	Norfolk
North Johnston	Pembrokeshire
Old Johnstone	Dumfriesshire

Peasedown St. John	Somerset
Sherborne St. John	Hampshire
St. John	Cornwall
St. Johns	Yorkshire
St. Johns	Warwickshire
St. Johns	Surrey
St. Johns	London
St. John's	Yorkshire
St. John's	Kent
St. John's	Worcestershire
St. John's Chapel	Durham
St. John's Chapel	Devon
St. John's Fen End	Norfolk
St. John's Highway	Norfolk
St. John's Park	Isle of Wight, Hampshire
St. John's Town of Dalry	Kirkcudbrightshire
St. John's Wood	Middlesex
Stanton St. John	Oxfordshire
Terrington St. John	Norfolk
Tipton St. John	Devon

THE ROAD TO JOHNS

There are five **John Streets** in London. One is a swanky
Bloomsbury address in WC1N, while another in E15 is a
more modest neighbourhood in London's East End. The
others are in Croydon, Enfield and Hounslow.

CELLULOID JOHNS

<u>Film character Johns</u>

Sylvester Stallone's Vietnam veteran **John Rambo** is one of the all-time classic American war heroes. We meet him in 1982's *First Blood* where his former Green Beret heroics and Medal of Honor count for little with anti-war folk.

In *Rambo First Blood: Part II*, he's removed from prison by his former superior officer for a top-secret operation to rescue POWs held in Vietnam. *Rambo III* – taglined 'God would have mercy, John Rambo won't!' – is set in Afghanistan where Sly's mission is to release his former commander from behind Soviet lines.

Richard Roundtree's **John Shaft** in *Shaft* (1971) was a tough cop dealing with Little Italy mobsters and Harlem gangsters. The catchy Theme From Shaft won an Oscar for Best Original Song.

The career of Bruce Willis took off when he played detective **John McClane** in the action movie *Die Hard* (1988). He has since cashed in with three sequels.

<u>Movie star Johns</u>

Johnny Depp was born John Christopher Depp in Kentucky in 1963 and dropped out of school in Florida at

15 to become a rock star. His band, The Kids, opened for
Iggy Pop, Duran Duran and the B-52s.

Depp made his film debut in *A Nightmare On Elm Street* in
1984 and his first title role was in *Edward Scissorhands*. He
won critical acclaim and commercial success in films such
as *Ed Wood*, *Donnie Brasco*, *Fear and Loathing in Las Vegas*,
Sleepy Hollow and the *Pirates of the Caribbean* series. He has
been nominated for three Oscars but, as of January 2009,
received none.

Depp plays lead slide guitar on the Oasis track Fade In-Out,
on the album Be Here Now because Noel Gallagher was
allegedly too drunk to do it himself. He co-owns a Tibetan
restaurant in Paris called *Man Ray* and has a nightclub,
Who Wouldn't Like Johnny Depp? named after him in Tartu,
Estonia.

John Cusack was born into a showbiz family in Illinois in
1966. He had worked on stage several times by the age of 12
and made his film debut at 17, appearing with Rob Lowe and
Andrew McCarthy in the romantic comedy *Class* (1983).

He started his own production company whose first movie
in 1997 was the sharp comedy *Grosse Pointe Blank* (1997), in
which he starred. In one of his least sensible career moves,
he turned down Woody Harrelson's role in *Indecent Proposal*.
One of his own favourite films is the surreal *Being John
Malkovich*.

John Malkovich (b. 1953) is an American actor best known for one of cinema's most bizarre hit movies, *Being John Malkovich*. The film centres on an office clerk's discovery of a 'portal' into Malkovich's mind, enabling paying customers to experience briefly life from the actor's point of view.

Publicity-shy Malkovich keeps a low profile and lived in the south of France for ten years where he worked in the theatre. He won an Emmy when appearing with Dustin Hoffman in a TV movie version of *Death of a Salesman* and was nominated for two Oscars for his roles in *Places of the Heart* and *In the Line of Fire*.

He's known for extreme right-wing views and held a Champagne party when serial killer John Wayne Gacy was executed. At the Cambridge Union in 2002, he said he "would like to shoot" pro-Palestinian journalist Robert Fisk and British MP George Galloway.

Actor **John Hannah**, born in Scotland in 1962, made his movie breakthrough as Matthew, the friend of Hugh Grant's who loses his gay lover in *Four Weddings and a Funeral* (1994). He tried his hand at acting after working for four years as a self-confessed "lazy electrician".

He was once turned down for a job at Pizza Express because he was not sufficiently "career-motivated". He went on to earn £500,000 for his role as Jonathan in *The Mummy Returns* (2001). His favourite Pizza Express pizza is the *Fiorentina*.

Born in New Jersey in 1954, **John Travolta** burst on to the big screen in the disco film *Saturday Night Fever* in 1977. After *Grease* and *Grease 2*, his career seemed to have fizzled out but he made a spectacular comeback in 1994 with an Oscar nomination for his stylish hitman in Quentin Tarantino's *Pulp Fiction*. He dressed up in drag and danced in high heels for his role as Edna Turnblad in the 2007 musical *Hairspray*.

Travolta is a fully qualified jet aircraft pilot, notably landing a Gulfstream IIB at Washington National Airport with complete electrical failure in icy conditions at night in 1993. He owns a Boeing 707.

John Hurt (b. 1940) is celebrated for his fine character-acting but in his best known screen roles and moments he is barely recognisable. In *Alien* (1979), his body hosts a predator who explodes from his stomach. In *The Elephant Man* the following year, he captured the pathetic personality of the disfigured Joseph Merrick, for which he won a BAFTA as best lead actor. He won a supporting actor BAFTA and Golden Globe for his performance in *Midnight Express*.

Sir John Gielgud's (1904-2000) extraordinary acting career spanned 76 years and he's one of only nine entertainers to have won an Oscar, a Grammy, an Emmy and a Tony, in standard categories. All of his Oscar and Emmy nominations came after he had turned 60. He received his Best Supporting Actor Oscar for his role as the butler in *Arthur 2*.

He was knighted in 1953, appointed a Companion of Honour in 1977, and made a member of the Order of Merit by the Queen for his exceptional contribution to the arts in 1996.

Sir John Mills, one of Britain's most loved actors, appeared in 120 films and TV movies between the 1932 *The Midshipmaid* and 2009's *The Snow Prince*.

He was the father of popular actresses Juliet Mills and Hayley Mills, and when he won an Oscar (supporting role) and a Golden Globe (supporting actor) for *Ryan's Daughter* (1970), he told reporters: "[It] is not my best film, but it is the best thing that happened to me, professionally. It brought me the Academy Award, and that meant I could finally be known again as somebody other than Hayley Mills' father."

He was appointed a CBE in 1960 and knighted in 1976. He came ninth in the 2001 Orange Film Survey of best British actors.

Stage Name	Real Name
John Derek	Derek Harris
John Forsythe	John Freund
John Garfield	Julius Garfinkle

Movies called John

There are two full-length movies titled *John*, neither of which is especially cheerful or successful. Roy Koriakin wrote and directed the dark comedy, *John*, about drug dealers in the 1990s.

In Vito Dinatolo's 2006 movie, *John*, a journalist wakes up with a dead girl. He plans to dispose of the body, but it disappears from his car on the way to work, and the day turns into a nightmare.

Movies with John in the title

D'Ye Ken John Peel? (1934)
Meet John Doe (1941)
The Great John L. (1945)
John Henry and the Inky-Poo (1946)
Captain John Smith and Pocahontas (1953)
Long John Silver (1954)
John Wesley (1954)
John and Julie (1955)
Alias John Preston (1955)
John Paul Jones (1959)
The John Glenn Story (1962)
I Think They Call Him John (1964)
John Goldfarb, Please Come Home (1965)
Oklahoma John (1965)
John Doe (1966)
John and Mary (1969)
An Impression of John Steinbeck: Writer (1969)
Scandalous John (1971)
Brother John (1971)

John and Marsha (1973)
Little Laura and Big John (1973)
The Legend of John Henry (1973)
Dear John (1987)
Imagine: John Lennon (1988)
Brother John (1988)
Big Bad John (1990)
There We Are, John (1993)
I Am John (1993)
Being John Malkovich (1999)
John Henry (2000)
The Search for John Gissing (2001)
Little John (2002)
A Day in the Life of John D. Impetus (2002)
Breaking with John (2004)
Day of John (2005)
The Killing of John Lennon (2006)
John Duffy's Brother (2006)
John Doe and the Anti (2006)
John Tucker Must Die (2006)
John Day Afternoon (2006)
The Treasures of Long Gone John (2006)
The Acquaintances of a Lonely John (2008)

Behind the Camera Johns

John Avildsen won a Best Director Oscar for the first
Rocky film in 1976. Other notable films include *Karate Kid I*,
II and *III*, *Rocky V* and *8 Seconds*.

He was due to direct *Saturday Night Fever* in 1977 but pulled
out at the last minute, to be replaced by John Badham,

John Badham, English-born son of actress Mary Hewitt, didn't really build on his big break to direct *Saturday Night Fever*. He won two Emmy awards for TV programmes and went on to direct *Dracula*, *Blue Thunder* and *WarGames*.

John Boorman (b. 1933) was a dry cleaner and an arts critic before working on TV documentaries for BBC Bristol. A friendship with Lee Marvin gave him his big break into Hollywood where he directed his friend in *Point Blank* (1967) and *Hell in the Pacific* (1968).

He wrote a 700-page script to film the three *Lord of the Rings* books as one movie in the 1970s but the project was foiled by studio politics. He won rave reviews for *Excalibur* and *The Emerald Forest* and received five Oscar nominations for his next two major films, *Deliverance* and the autobiographical *Hope and Glory*.

He has yet to win an Oscar despite receiving 17 major film prizes and 23 further nominations.

Horror, thriller and sci-fi director **John Carpenter**'s films include *Halloween*, *The Fog*, *Escape from New York*, *Village of the Vampires* and *Ghosts of Mars*. His tendency to avoid showing gore has put him out of step with the modern horror trends of slasher movies. His favourite meal is breakfast which he eats at any time of the day.

Legendary Hollywood film-maker **John Ford** (1894-1973) directed his first major feature, *The Secret Man*, in 1917, and his last, *7 Women*, in 1966. In between, he made some of the world's most popular movies, including *Stagecoach* (1939), *She Wore a Yellow Ribbon* (1949), *Rio Grande* (1950), *The Quiet Man* (1952), *Mogambo* (1953), *The Searchers* (1956) and *The Man Who Shot Liberty Vallance* (1962).

He was the first director to win back-to-back Best Director Oscars for *The Grapes of Wrath* (1940) and *How Green Was My Valley* (1941). He won a further two Academy awards.

Orson Welles repeatedly watched *Stagecoach* before directing his first film, *Citizen Kane* (1941). When he was asked to name his three favourite directors, Welles answered: "John Ford, John Ford and John Ford."

When Ford died aged 79 in 1973, he was widely regarded as the best American film director of all time.

John Huston (1906-1987) was another movie legend with a prodigious output of iconic films, including *The Maltese Falcon* (1941), *In This Our Life* (1942), *Key Largo* (1948), *The Treasure of the Sierra Madre* (1948), *The Asphalt Jungle* (1950), *The African Queen* (1951), *Moby Dick* (1956), *The Misfits* (1961),*The Night of the Iguana* (1964), *The Life and Times of Judge Roy Bean* (1972), *Prizzi's Honor* (1985) and *The Dead* (1987).

Huston won two Oscars and 35 other awards. He's the only person to have directed a parent (Walter Huston) and a child (Anjelica Huston) to Oscar wins. Huston is also one of few to receive at least one Oscar nomination in five consecutive decades, from the 1940s to 1980s.

John Lasseter co-wrote and directed the first full-length animated feature created with computer graphics. He won a special achievement Oscar for the 1995 film, *Toy Story*, having received an Animated Short Film Oscar for *Tin Toy* in 1988.

Lasseter's many films include, as director: *A Bug's Life* (1998), *Toy Story 2* (1999), *Cars* (2006) and *Toy Story 3* (2008). He was also executive producer on film hits: *Monsters, Inc.* (2001), *Finding Nemo* (2003), *The Incredibles* (2004) and *Ratatouille* (2007).

British director **John Schlesinger** won the Best Director Oscar for his 1969 movie *Midnight Cowboy*, which also won the Best Picture Oscar and is widely regarded as a modern classic. He made 18 major films in a 38-year career, including *A Kind of Loving* (1962), *Billy Liar* (1963), *Far from the Madding Crowd* (1967), *Sunday, Bloody Sunday* (1971), *Marathon Man* (1976), *Yanks* (1979), *The Believers* (1987), *Cold Comfort Farm* (1995), and *The Next Best Thing* (2000).

It's incredible that director **John Sturges** (1911-1952) received just one Oscar nomination, for *Bad Day at Black Rock* (1955), and no wins for the many successful films he directed. His big-budget action movies include such classics as *Gunfight at the O.K. Corral* (1957), *The Magnificent*

Seven (1960), *The Great Escape* (1963), *The Satan Bug* (1965), *Ice Station Zebra* (1968), and *The Eagle Has Landed* (1976).

FIGHTING JOHNS

Welshman **John Chambers** wrote the Marquess of Queensberry Rules, in 1867, on which modern boxing is based. Among these were the required use of boxing gloves, the ten-count, three-minute rounds and a one-minute break between rounds. Chambers stipulated the ring size at 24 ft (7.3m) square.

No seconds or any other person were to be allowed in the ring during the rounds and fighters were not allowed to wear shoes or boots with springs. The rules were named after **John Douglas**, a Scottish nobleman and the ninth Marquess of Queensberry, who was Chambers' sponsor.

John Sullivan (1858–1918) became bare-knuckle world champion in 1883 when he beat Briton Charley Mitchell in France. The following year he knocked out challenger Jake Kilrain in round 75 of a scheduled 80-round bout, the last ever world title fight without gloves.

At the end of a bloody, two-hour rematch with Mitchell at a chateau in Chantilly, France, in 1888, police arrested Mitchell as boxing was illegal in that country. Sullivan escaped and hired his old foe to work in his corner for many years.

Sullivan was the first gloved boxing champion of the world, the first national American sports hero, and the first athlete to earn more than £500,000.

Male under-garment **Long Johns** are said to be named after Sullivan who boxed in long underpants.

Liverpool-born **John Conteh** was one of Britain's most successful boxers. At 19, he won the middleweight gold medal in the 1970 British Commonwealth Games and gained the WBC light heavyweight title in October 1974, holding the crown until 1978 when it was taken away for his refusal of a mandatory defence.

He retired from boxing in 1980 with a professional record of 34 wins, 1 draw, and 4 losses.

Conteh was the second winner of the televised *British Superstars* competition in 1974, beating Olympic gold medallist David Hemery and England footballer Colin Bell in the final.

Conteh has admitted that a partying lifestyle caused the premature end of his career. He appeared in the TV show *Boon* in 1989, as a washed-up boxer.

John H. Stracey (b. 1950) was British, European and world welterweight champion who retired with a career record of 45 wins (including 37 knockouts), five defeats and one draw.

Stracey trained Gary and Martin Kemp to box for six months for the film *The Krays*. He also choreographed the boxing scenes, acclaimed by the critics as the most authentic fight scenes ever used in a British film.

He now tours with stories of his East End upbringing and exploits in the ring, taking his cherished World Title Belt to each event.

John Owens, commonly known as **Johnny Owens** was the fourth of eight children in a working class family from South Wales. He was known as 'The Matchstick Man' due to his wiry frame and 'The Bionic Skeleton' for his amazing strength and stamina.

He went on to become Welsh, British, Commonwealth and European champion at bantamweight but is best remembered for his failed attempt to take the world title from Mexican Lupe Pintor in Los Angeles in September 1980.

Johnny was ahead on points after nine rounds but took punishment in the 10th and 11th. Pintor knocked Owens out in the 12th and he was taken from the ring to hospital where he lay in a coma until November 4th 1980 when he lost his final fight – for his life. He was just 24 years old.

COCKNEY RHYMING JOHNS

Cockney rhyming slang is formed by two related words with the first standing for a word that rhymes with the second.

Examples include 'Julius' (Julius Caesar) for geezer and 'Jurassic' (Jurassic Park) for dark.

John Cleese – Cheese
John Deut – Beaut (beauty)
John Hop – Cop (policeman)
John Major – Pager
John Major – Wager
John Skinner – Dinner
John Wayne – Train
John West – Best
Johnnie Rutter – Butter
Johnny Cash – Slash (urinate)

GRANGE HILL JOHNS

John Alford (b. 1971) who played angel-faced schoolboy Robbie Wright, was enjoying one of the most successful post-*Grange Hill* careers with a leading role in ITV's *London's Burning* and even featuring on two top 20 chart singles. But he was jailed for nine months for supplying cocaine and cannabis after a sting by the *News of the World*'s famous 'fake sheikh'.

He now drives a taxi in north London.

John Pickard has followed up his part of *Grange Hill*'s Neil Timpson with appearances in Channel 4's *Hollyoaks*, playing Dominic Reilly. He had a leading role playing David Porter in the 1990s sitcom *2point4 Children* and from 1993-1996 was Kevin, the sidekick of Robbie Jackson (Dean Gaffney), in BBC's *EastEnders*.

John Drummond played the ginger, overweight bully, Trevor Cleaver, who stole youngsters' dinner money and drank lager in Series 8. He had previously played a boy called Barry from the neighbouring school, Rodney Bennett, in Series 6.

⟫◆⟪

FUNNY JOHNS

John Marwood Cleese (b. 1939) co-founder of *Monty Python's Flying Circus* and creator of *Fawlty Towers*, would have been known as John Cheese if his dad Reg, an insurance salesman, hadn't changed his surname to avoid taunting when he joined the army.

The Python adventure happened because Cleese turned down the chance of a series with Graham Chapman, due to his co-writer's alcoholism. Cleese invited Michael Palin who in turn insisted on Terry Jones and Eric Idle joining the team in 1969.

Cleese didn't feature in the fourth and last TV series as he thought the Pythons had run out of steam but he returned for the film hits *Monty Python and the Holy Grail*, *Life of Brian* and *The Meaning of Life*.

He masterminded the first Amnesty International charity show, *The Secret Policeman's Ball*, and set up a training company, Video Arts, which he and three co-founders sold for £42million. He has a species of lemur, *Avahi clees,i*, and an asteroid, *9618 Johncleese*, named after him.

John Sullivan (b. 1946), creator and writer of TV's smash hit sitcom *Only Fools and Horses*, seemed destined for factory life until he bumped into old school friend, Paul Saunders, in his job at Watneys brewery.

The BBC turned down the friends' sitcom idea but John so enjoyed writing that he joined the corporation as a scenery shifter to boost his chances.

Ronnie Barker gave him his first break on *The Two Ronnies* but his big chance came when he penned a *Citizen Smith* episode for the BBC's Comedy Playhouse season, leading to four series starring Robert Lindsay as the Tooting revolutionary, Wolfie Smith.

Only Fools and Horses' original 1981 rating of 7.7 million viewers was modest but when 25.3 million people watched a Christmas special in 1996, it was – and still is – the biggest ever audience for a sitcom episode on British television.

Sullivan invented the wonderful Del Boy Trotter and added colourful words to the English language, including 'plonker', 'cushty' and 'lovely jubbly'.

Fellow Cockney **Johnny Speight** had been John Sullivan's inspiration. Speight, born John Speight in 1920 in West Ham, created one of British culture's most enduring and controversial comedy characters, Alf Garnett, who was masterfully played by Warren Mitchell.

Alf's racist and reactionary views in *Till Death Us Do Part* were based on those of Speight's father, whose attitudes had upset his son.

Alf's catchphrase "silly moo" came about after BBC bosses asked him to stop calling her a "cow". The original series ran for 10 years from 1965 but the character lived until 1992 through two sequels, *Till Death...* and *In Sickness and in Health*.

John Inman (1935-2007) became a national treasure in his role of the camp Mr. Humphries in the department store sitcom *Are You Being Served?* The show ran from 1972 to 1985 and with his catchphrase "I'm free" and a mincing walk, Inman was one of TV comedy's first openly homosexual characters.

Gay rights activists condemned his stereotypical performance but the public loved him. He was voted funniest man on television by readers of *TV Times* magazine in 1976 when he was also BBC TV's personality of the year. In later years, he earned a handsome living as a stage actor, becoming one of the UK's favourite pantomime dames.

The on-stage characters of **Jilted John** and **John Shuttleworth** were created by Sheffield-born comedian Graham Fellows (b. 1959). Jilted John had a novelty hit single of the same name in 1978. The punk-style record told how John's girlfriend Julie had left him for a chap named Gordon, "but I know he's a moron, Gordon is a moron".

It reached number four in the charts but was probably not purchased by many people called Gordon.

A decade later, Fellows created 50-something singer-songwriter Shuttleworth, who performed on a squeaky portable keyboard, completely oblivious to his lack of talent.

In 2007, he toured a stage show *With My Condiments*, based on chef Jamie Oliver's healthy school meals campaign. His most recent release, 4 Tasty Tracks, was recorded in a wardrobe and reached number 96 in the charts.

John Thomson (b. 1969) grew up near Preston, where he became friends with fellow comedian Steve Coogan, (later appearing as Fat Bob in *Paul Calf* sketches). He wrote and appeared in the TV sketch series, *The Fast Show*, with smooth jazz presenter Louis Balfour his most memorable character.

He has also appeared as Pete Gifford in ITV's hit comedy *Cold Feet*. He is reported to have scored 168 in an IQ test and to be nicknamed 'Google' by colleagues because he's such a know-all.

John Moloney was voted Best Live Performer for two years running at the London Comedy Festival. He was a writer on the award-winning *Jack Dee Show* in London's West End and was nominated by the Comedy Store in the category Best Live Stand-Up at the British Comedy Awards.

John Hegley (b. 1953) is that rarest of animals – a professional poet, albeit a comedy one. After working as a bus conductor in Bristol, he studied literature and sociology at Bradford University before returning to his home city of London to earn money busking and in children's theatre.

His five books of poetry include *Glad to Wear Glasses* (1990) and *Love Cuts* (1995). An example of his offbeat style is:

The difference between dogs and sheds:
It's not a very good idea to give a dog
a coat
of creosote

John Belushi was born in Chicago in 1949, the son of an Albanian immigrant restaurant owner. He moved to New York to join an unpromising off-Broadway rock music revue *National Lampoon's Lemmings*, for a six-week run.

The show played to full houses for ten months.

His big break came in 1975 with the hit TV series *Saturday Night Live* where film director John Landis spotted him and cast him in his *National Lampoon's Animal House* movie. Landis gave John and *Saturday Night Live* colleague Dan Aykroyd the title roles in *The Blues Brothers* movie where they became international stars.

Belushi married his childhood sweetheart Judy but his was to be no Hollywood happy ending. He was found dead from a lethal injection of cocaine and heroin in a hotel room on Sunset Boulevard in March 1982. He was 33.

INNOVATIVE JOHNS

After 2,000 Englishmen died in 1707 when ships ran aground in fog in the Scilly Isles, the government offered £20,000 to anyone who could calculate longitude at sea. (Latitude was calculated by the position of the sun and stars.)

Working-class Lincolnshire joiner **John Harrison** (1693-1776) worked out that the earth rotated one degree of longitude every four minutes. He created a clock to keep accurate time of the home port, allowing mariners to work out longitude.

The government refused to pay out, saying his solution was a fluke, but he was eventually paid by parliamentary decree after an intervention by King George III.

Harrison's story was told dramatically by Dava Sobel in her book *Longitude*. The surprise best-seller was made into a 2000 film of the same name featuring Michael Gambon as Harrison.

In 1731, **John Hadley** and Thomas Godfrey independently invented the reflecting quadrant, a precursor to the sextant to measure latitude. Royal Naval Captain John Campbell's sextant, invented in 1757, could measure both longitude and latitude.

Bad health forced Scotsman **John Logie Baird** to abandon his business selling jam in the Caribbean and he retired aged 34. In a bare attic in Hastings, Sussex, the penniless Baird built the world's first TV contraption out of a tea-chest, washstand, a projection lamp, biscuit tin, cardboard disks and lenses from bicycle lamps. The device was held together by scrap wood, darning needles, string, and sealing-wax.

He transmitted the image of a Maltese Cross over a few feet in 1924. Two years later, he demonstrated TV before fifty scientists in Frith Street, Soho. In 1927, he revealed colour TV and stereo sound in a transmission from London to New York. His equipment is preserved in the Science Museum, London.

Some of Baird's early inventions were less successful. In his 20s, he shorted out Glasgow's entire electricity supply when he tried to create diamonds by heating graphite. He also perfected a glass razor which was rust-resistant – but, unsurprisingly, shattered. He tried to make pneumatic shoes but his prototype containing semi-inflated balloons burst.

In a recent TV (where else?) interview, Baird's son Malcolm said if his father had known what type of rubbish would be broadcast sixty years later, he would not have bothered with the invention. But who could have foreseen Richard and Judy in the 1920s?

John MacAdam (1756-1836) was appointed surveyor to the Bristol Turnpike Trust in 1816 and remade roads under his control with a new method using crushed stone bound with gravel. A camber made the road slightly convex so the rainwater drained off quickly.

The success of the so-called Macadamised system led to his becoming surveyor-general of metropolitan roads in England. Most European main roads in Europe were built this way by the end of the 19th century.

Scotsman **John Napier** (1550-1617) invented logarithms as a system to simplify large, difficult calculations and the decimal point to express fractions in the metric system. But he believed his book predicting the end of the world in 1688 or 1700 was his most important work. He never found out that he was wrong.

John Dunlop qualified at Edinburgh Veterinary College at 19 and worked as a vet in the city for ten years before moving to Belfast. He found the rough Irish roads and iron, wood or solid rubber wheels to be uncomfortable so he experimented with his son's tricycle to come up with an inflated rubber tube which he patented in 1888.

He created the Dunlop Rubber Company but had to win a legal battle with fellow Scot Robert William Thomson who claimed to have made the same invention. John Dunlop didn't benefit financially from his invention – he sold the patent and company name for a modest sum – but was credited with the invention of the rubber tyre.

Professor **John Atanasoff** and student Clifford Berry built the world's first electronic-digital computer at Iowa State University between 1939 and 1942, based on Atanasoff's conceptual drawings on the back of a cocktail napkin (he was fond of fast cars and Scottish whisky). The computer's innovations included a binary system of processing and separation of memory and computing functionality.

The computer was the size of a desk, weighed 700 lb (318 kg), and contained more than 300 vacuum tubes and a mile of wire. It calculated one operation every 15 seconds compared with 10 billion a second by today's PCs. The Atanasoff-Berry computer was lost to posterity when it was dismantled because the university needed more space in its physics building.

English engraver and mapmaker, **John Spilsbury**, invented the jigsaw puzzle in 1767. He attached a world map to a piece of wood and cut out each country, enabling teachers to use his puzzles to teach geography.

In the early 1890s, English geologist and mining engineer **John Milne** developed the first accurate seismograph to record ground shaking during earthquakes, a frequent occurrence in Japan where he worked.

English chemist, **John Walker**, discovered in 1827 that if he coated the end of a stick with certain chemicals and let them dry, he could start a fire by striking the stick anywhere. The chemicals used in these early matches were antimony sulfide, potassium chlorate, gum, and starch.

Walker did not patent his 'Congreves' as he called the matches (named after Congreve's rocket system invented in 1808). He made his first sale of his new product on April 7th 1827, to a Mr. Hixon, a solicitor in Stockton-on-Tees. Walker had made little money from his invention when he died in 1859, aged 78.

Scientist **John Lilly** built the first sensory deprivation tank in 1954 to find out what happened when the brain was cut off from external stimuli. Lilly experienced vivid fantasies as he floated in warm water for hours in darkness and silence.

The hallucinations were "too personal to relate publicly" and he scrapped scientific research to make a tidy income selling appliances through his firm Samadhi Tanks. The 1980 film *Altered States*, starring William Hurt, was based on his work.

———◆———

CLEVER JOHNS

Eton and Cambridge-educated **John Maynard Keynes** changed the face of economics and many governments' economic policy agendas with his classic book, *The General Theory of Employment, Interest and Money*, in 1936. No other book has had such a major impact on the role of government in the economy.

Keynes theorised that the determining factor of total output and employment was aggregate demand and that governments could eradicate unemployment by ensuring the level of demand remained in balance.

Keynesian economics fell out of favour from 1980 until recently, but the 2008 credit crunch and banking crisis has seen a marked revival of his ideas and fiscal policies.

John Nash (b. 1928) is an American mathematician, who was diagnosed with paranoid schizophrenia and clinical depression in 1959 while still at college. In spite of the illness, he continued his studies and won the John von Neumann Theory Prize, the Leroy P. Steel Prize and the prestigious Nobel Prize in 1994.

A film based on his life, *A Beautiful Mind*, was released in 2001, starring Russell Crowe, and won four Oscars, including Best Picture.

John Ramsay, a sixth-form student at Wirral Grammar School for Boys, gained an incredible six 'A' grade A-Levels in 2008. John is following a Master's course in engineering at Birmingham University.

Aeronautical engineer **John Dunne** (1875-1949) designed military aircraft and was a soldier in the Second Boer War, serving on two tours of duty in 1900 and 1902. But his most fascinating work was on the nature of time, prompted by his premonition in a dream of the 1902 eruption of Mount Pelée in Martinique.

Dunne's experiments led him to believe that our experience of time as linear was an illusion, and that past, present and future were simultaneous, and experienced as a sequence of events only because of our mental perception of them.

He said people could access a different view of time whilst dreaming. The theory expounded in his books, *An Experiment with Time* (1927) and *The Serial Universe* (1934), influenced writers such as Aldous Huxley and J. B. Priestley.

CORPORATE JOHN

Born in 1885, **John Spedan Lewis** was the son of John,
who opened the John Lewis department store in Oxford
Street in the early 1900s.

After taking over the running of the store in 1914, and
whilst recovering from a horse-riding accident, John
reflected that he, his brother and father between them
enjoyed earnings equal to those of their entire workforce.
He started to offer staff much better pay and conditions but
his father disagreed with his policies and the two fell out.

At the company's Peter Jones shop, the son's enlightened
approach turned a sizeable deficit into a huge profit in five
years. When his father died in 1928, Lewis acted so that
profits were distributed among employees and, 21 years
later, he made the John Lewis Partnership the property of
its workers.

By 2007, 69,000 permanent staff owned 27 John Lewis
department stores, 198 Waitrose supermarkets, an online
and catalogue business, johnlewis.com, direct services
company, Greenbee, a production unit and a farm – with a
combined turnover of nearly £6.8 billion.

FOOD AND DRINK JOHNS

The world's most popular fast food was invented late one night in 1762 when hungry English nobleman, **John Montagu, the Fourth Earl of Sandwich**, was too busy gambling to stop for a meal. He asked a waiter for roast-beef between two slices of bread so he wouldn't get his fingers greasy whilst playing cards.

Pharmacist Doctor **John Pemberton** (1831-1888) invented Coca-Cola in a brass kettle in his Atlanta, Georgia, back garden in 1886, selling his first drink in the city's Jacob's Pharmacy, on May 8th that year.

Pemberton actually lost money in his first year of sales with £35 of expenses more than wiping out £25 of sales.

The drink was originally marketed as a tonic and contained cocaine and the caffeine-strong kola nut until 1905. The name and famous lettering were provided by Pemberton's book-keeper, Frank Robinson, who just happened to have nice handwriting.

Worcestershire chemists **John Wheeley Lea** (1791-1874) and William Henry Perrins invented Worcestershire Sauce by accident after being asked by Lord Marcus Sandys, the former governor of Bengal, to create a fish sauce.

Their anchovy-based effort was horrible and they left the concoction in their cellar, forgetting about it until they came across it two years later. When they tasted it they found that it had matured to develop an aromatic, pleasant flavour. The pair started producing Lea & Perrins Original Worcestershire Sauce in 1837.

They arranged that all restaurants on ocean liners to and from England carried the condiment and paid waiters to sell it to passengers. The sauce is sold in round bottles because the original vessels had been chemist's medicine bottles.

The Bloody Mary cocktail was born in 1921, when Fernand Petiot, a barman at trendy Harry's New York Bar in Paris added Worcestershire Sauce to vodka and tomato juice.

Dr. John Kellogg and younger brother Will formed the Sanitas Food Company in Michigan in 1897 to produce whole grain cereals. In those times the standard breakfast for the wealthy was eggs and meat while the poor ate porridge or gruel.

The pair invented cornflakes but later argued over the recipe. Will wanted to add sugar and in 1906 started his own company, the Battle Creek Toasted Corn Flake Company, which eventually became the Kellogg Company. His move started a long feud and John left the firm to create the Battle Creek Food Company, making soy products.

John was an earnest campaigner for sexual abstinence and devoted considerable energy to discourage sexual activity, believing that even within marriage sexual 'excesses' could lead to physical, moral and psychological problems.

Although he and his wife Ella were married for over 40 years, they never had sexual intercourse and had separate bedrooms all their lives.

Kellogg's most zealous campaigning was against masturbation, claiming that practice of this 'solitary-vice' caused cancer of the womb, urinary diseases, nocturnal emissions, impotence, epilepsy, insanity, and mental and physical debility as well 'dimness of vision'.

Kellogg worked on the rehabilitation of masturbators. He recommended applying pure carbolic acid to the female genitals as a way of 'allaying the abnormal excitement' and, for boys, the bandaging of hands and covering genitals with cages.

In his 90s, John decided to heal the rift with Will and wrote him a letter, but his secretary thought it demeaned him and did not send it.

Will read the letter after John's death.

John Cadbury sold the first boxes of chocolates in 1868 in Birmingham. His new process for pressing cocoa butter from cocoa beans transformed his small family business, Cadbury Brothers, into a global giant now known as Cadbury Schweppes.

The summer cocktail **John Collins** was invented by the head waiter at Limmer's hotel and coffee shop in London, in the late 1790s. His original version used *genever*, a Dutch-style gin, soda water, lemon and sugar.

The cocktail became popular in the USA and when a bartender there used Old Tom, a London gin, it became known as a Tom Collins.

For some reason, a Collins made with bourbon or whisky was given the name John Collins. The cocktail gave rise to many variations, such as Brandy Collins, Jack Collins (apple brandy), Mike Collins (Irish whiskey), Pedro Collins (Rum) and Vodka Collins. Most serious cocktail bars will serve these in a traditional Collins highball glass.

To make a John Collins take one shot of bourbon, two teaspoons of icing sugar or sugar syrup, four shots of lemon juice, and soda to taste. Mix everything together, except the soda, shake with ice and pour into a tall glass. Top up with soda.

John Dory, also known as St. Pierre or St. Peter's Fish, is an extremely edible deep-sea fish found at the bottom of the Indian and Atlantic Oceans, and in the Mediterranean Sea.

Its scientific name is *Zeus faber* and its olive-yellow body has a large dark spot on each side. Explanations for its name range from the French *dorée*, meaning golden, or *jaune* (yellow), or John Dory, the hero of an old folk ballad.

The John Dory grows to a maximum size of 2ft 1in (65cm) and 6.6lb (3kg). According to the Food and

Agriculture Organisation of the United Nations,
the John Dory is "a poor swimmer", surely a serious
disadvantage for a fish?

It is, however, "the top predator in its habitat".

⟩⟨

HOAXER JOHNS

A front page article by the *New York Sun* in August 1835
listed a series of amazing breakthroughs by British
astronomer, **Sir John Herschel**, using a unique, and very
large, telescope. Herschel was reported to have discovered
planets in other star systems and intelligent life on the
moon.

Sir John described forests, seas, and lilac-coloured pyramids
on the lunar surface where bison wandered the plains and
blue unicorns lived on hilltops. The article was, of course,
a hoax and Herschel was not even aware of many of the
discoveries attributed to him.

His real claim to immortality is the word 'photography',
a term he coined in a paper entitled *Note on the Art of
Photography*, or *The Application of the Chemical Rays of
Light to the Purpose of Pictorial Representation*, presented to
the Royal Society in 1839. He also created the terms
'negative' and 'positive' for photographs, as well as
'snapshot'.

John Humble (b. 1956), the man who taunted police during the Yorkshire Ripper's reign of terror, was jailed for eight years after falsely claiming to be the murderer in three letters and an audio tape. His hoaxes led police to focus their hunt in Sunderland while the Ripper carried on killing in Yorkshire.

Humble, 50, of Sunderland, admitted four charges of perverting the course of justice. Judge Norman Jones said real killer Peter Sutcliffe told police the letters and tape had given him "confidence".

In 2000, a man calling himself TimeTravel_0, and later **John Titor**, started posting on a public forum that he was a time traveller from the future. He uploaded pictures and the operations manual of his "time machine".

On March 21st 2001, John Titor said he was returning to 2036 and was never heard of again. Many readers felt Titor's predictions and comments seemed to be coming true. His posts were written before 9/11 and the second Gulf War, and many people believe Titor had left clues about these events without actually referring to them.

It's widely agreed that he made several predictions about physics discoveries that have since materialised. But he must have been a hoaxer... surely?

WHAT DOES JOHNNY MEAN, EXACTLY?

The terms Johnny or **Rubber Johnny** are used as slang for a condom. The best explanation for this seems to be that a condom is a rubber item man placed over a man's John Thomas (slang for his male member) or Johnny.

⟹◆⟸

SCANDALOUS JOHNS

Old Etonian Tory Minister **John Profumo** (1915-2006) was at the centre of one of British politics' biggest sex scandals, causing him to resign from Harold Macmillan's government in 1963.

The Secretary of State for War admitted he'd lied to Parliament about his relationship with Christine Keeler, a call-girl who had also been seeing Russian naval attaché and spy, Yevgeny Ivanov. The affair was a factor in the Conservatives' General Election defeat the following year.

Instead of seeking sympathy, he spent 40 years working for Toynbee Hall, a charity helping down-and-outs in the East End of London. He was appointed CBE in 1975 on the advice of Labour Prime Minister Harold Wilson.

When the film about the affair, *Scandal*, came out in 1989, Profumo and his wife Valerie, who had stood by him, were due to be guests at a dinner for the Queen Mother. They offered not to attend, but the Queen Mother insisted they came

John DeLorean set out to create an 'ethical' sports car and based his factory near Belfast, tempted by £40 million of British government funding.

The DeLorean was a strange, rear-engined two-seater, with an innovative plastic chassis and winged doors that made it look like a bird in flight when both were open.

But it had little power and was expensive at £12,500.

The workforce had no car manufacturing experience and DeLorean had to build factories in the USA to fix the many mistakes they made. More than £77 million of taxpayers' money had been pumped into the company when DeLorean declared it insolvent.

A Michigan grand jury decided that £8.25 million had found its way into the hands of DeLorean and his cronies via a Panama firm. DeLorean wriggled out of an extradition request to the USA and the only time he spent in jail was 10 days on a charge of smuggling cocaine worth £12 million.

A few of the cars survive as collectors' items. They also transported Michael J. Fox in the *Back to The Future* movies.

John Rusnak lost Allfirst Bank of Baltimore, a subsidiary of the Allied Irish Bank, £493 million in a scandal unveiled in 2002. He covered up trading setbacks while throwing away more cash in an effort to recoup debts. He hid the losses from his bosses and didn't even tell his wife what was happening.

When his bank sent executives on a Friday to investigate suspect trades, 37-year-old Rusnak simply failed to go to work on Monday. Rusnak was sentenced to seven and a half years in prison for fraud. He could have faced up to 30 years in prison but his sentence was shortened as part of a plea bargain with prosecutors.

He was released to home confinement in September 2008 and was freed in January 2009 after serving less than six years. He is now paying £715 a month for five years.

He will remain liable for the full £493 million he lost but the amount he pays back will depend on how much money he earns in future.

LOSING JOHNS

The 72-year-old **John McCain** would have been the oldest man to become USA President if he had beaten Barack Obama in the 2008 election. Republican McCain's 58.42 million votes (46% of the total) was comfortably beaten by Democrat Obama's 67.7 million (53%).

After fighting a fierce campaign, McCain was generous to his rival in his concession speech: "In a contest as long and difficult as this campaign has been, his success alone commands my respect for his ability and perseverance. But that he managed to do so by inspiring the hopes of so many millions of Americans who had once wrongly believed that they had little at stake or little influence in the election of an American president is something I deeply admire and commend him for achieving."

McCain was elected to the US Senate in 1986 after a military career that saw him tortured by the North Vietnamese in the infamous 'Hanoi Hilton' prison.

The Democrats' 2003 presidential candidate **John Kerry** (b. 1943) was a war hero with three Purple Hearts and many other medals. But his experience of war in two Vietnam tours of duty shocked him, especially the number of soldiers who died because of bad decisions by military planners, and he became an anti-war protester when he returned home.

He was beaten by George W. Bush in November 2004 by the narrowest of margins in the race for the White House. Kerry won 59.03 million votes (48 per cent) and Bush 62.04 million (51 per cent).

UNWELL JOHNS

Millions of dieters would love to contract the illness plaguing **John Perry**. Born in the late 1940s, he eats whatever he likes without getting overweight due to a condition called lipodystrophy that makes him rapidly burn fat.

Perry eats takeaways, chips, chocolate and clotted cream, but his weight remains 11st 12lb.

He was a chubby child but at 12 the fat dropped off "almost overnight". After a decade of tests, the illness was diagnosed when doctors discovered his body produced six times the normal level of insulin. Doctors say the condition would be a "slimmer's dream".

Arthur and **John Mowforth** were twins who lived 80 miles apart in the UK. On the evening of May 22nd 1975, both fell severely ill from chest pains. The families of both men were unaware of the other's illness. The pair were rushed to separate hospitals at approximately the same time.

And both died of heart attacks shortly after arrival.

RECORD-BREAKING JOHNS

UK strongman **John Evans** has 32 Guinness World Records and 34 Record Holders Republic World Records.

In 2007, at 60 years old, he broke two of his own records, balancing 429 full cans of 7-Up on his head for 15 seconds (a weight of 27 stone or 171 kg) and 98 milk crates for 10 seconds.

He carried a 352 lb (159.6 kg) Mini car on his head for 33 seconds at The London Studios in May 1999.

John Davidson of Lincolnshire, claimed a new world record for eating Yorkshire Puddings by scoffing 3 lb (1.36 kg) worth plus half a pint (0.25 of a litre) of onion gravy in seven minutes, 22 seconds in March 1986.

The world champion pizza eating record holder is **John Kenmuir** of Hamilton who ate a 2 lb (1.27 kg) pizza in 29 seconds at the Glasgow Garden Festival in August 1988. A year earlier he ate 14 hard-boiled eggs in 14.2 seconds on Scottish TV's *Live at 1.30*.

John Kassar lay on a bed of six-inch nails, a wooden board was placed on his chest and 29 girls climbed on to it on BBC TV's *Late, Late Breakfast Show* in 1983.

The total weight pressing down on John's body was a world record 3,638 lb (1,650 kg). His body was marked but the sharp nails didn't penetrate his skin.

ACCIDENTAL JOHNS

The Shadows' bassist **John Rostill** was electrocuted by his guitar in his home recording studio in 1973.

American **John Wayne Bobbit** (b. 1967) made international headlines in 1993 when his wife, Lorena, cut off his penis, drove off into the night and threw it in a field. She dialled 911 and his member was found, packed in ice and reattached during nine hours of surgery.

He formed a band The Severed Parts to raise money to pay for the surgery and legal bills, and cashed in on his notoriety by appearing in several porn films including *John Wayne Bobbit Uncut* and *John Wayne Bobbitt's Frankenpenis*.

His wife, meanwhile, was found not guilty after accusing Bobbit of abuse and infidelity during her trial.

John Kennedy Jr., the third child and first son of President John F. Kennedy and Jacqueline Kennedy, died at the age of 38 with his wife and sister-in-law when a light aircraft he was flying crashed into the Atlantic on his way to Martha's Vineyard, off the USA's east coast, in 1999. A controversial researcher of alien abductions was killed when hit by a car in a London street. **John E. Mack**, a Pulitzer Prize-winning author and Harvard Medical School psychiatry professor, was widely criticised for asserting that abductions were probably real experiences, albeit spiritual rather than physical ones. His best-selling book, *Abduction,* was published in 1994 and based on interviews with more than 200 people who claimed to have had encounters with extraterrestrials.

Celtic and Scotland goalkeeper **John Thomson** died at the age of 22 after a serious head injury while playing against Rangers at Ibrox on Saturday September 5th 1931. Thomson was a brave goalkeeper whose dive at the feet of Sam English led to a full impact of the forward's knee on his head.

More than 40,000 people attended his funeral. The epitaph on his gravestone reads:

"They never die who live in the hearts they leave behind."

American rhythm and blues singer, **Johnny Ace**, died aged 25, during a backstage break during his gig at the Houston City Auditorium in 1954. He thought he was pretending to have a game of Russian roulette. But the gun was loaded and he killed himself after firing two blank shots at his girlfriend and another woman.

Born John Marshall Alexander, Jr. in Memphis, Tennessee, he served in the US Navy during the Korean War and then had a great career break when was hired to play in blues legend B. B. King's band. As Johnny Ace, he had nine solo hits between 1952 and 1954. But his biggest seller, Pledging My Love, became a hit after his death.

After surf-fishing on Crystal Beach, Texas, **a driver named John** curled up for forty winks underneath his truck, parked on the beach. The next morning, a pickup truck was reported abandoned in the surf.

A tow truck driver had barely moved the pickup, when he found the body of a 37-year-old man embedded in the sand beneath it. The truck had not been abandoned, after all. As John slept, time passed and the tide rolled back in. The wet sand shifted beneath the truck's weight, and he was trapped beneath it, unable to escape.

At least he won a 2005 Darwin Award:

Honouring those who improve the species... by accidentally removing themselves from it.

An 'Honourable Mention' in the 2007 Darwins was received by a **22-year-old John** in the USA who answered his friend's call for barbecue coal by loading his already burning grill on to his trusty 1978 Chevrolet pickup truck.

Hot charcoal met propane tank. The tank exploded and the Chevy was engulfed in flames. John escaped with burns to his lower legs so avoided a Darwin nomination.

"Obviously, we would urge people not to drive with burning grills in their vehicles," a Sheriff's Office spokesman said.

In an unconfirmed 2007 Darwin nomination, a British man named **John**, 71, used wood and rope to make a clever traction device to ease his wife's neck pain.

Guess what happened when he tested it? Yes, he hanged himself.

The coroner's verdict: death by misadventure.

RULING JOHNS

England has had only one **King John**, who was born in 1166 and reigned from 1199 until his death in 1216. He was generally regarded as one of the worst monarchs and a weak, greedy king.

He refused to pay a ransom when his brother, King Richard the Lionheart, was kidnapped, was in constant dispute with legendary outlaw Robin Hood and was forced to sign in 1215 the *Magna Carta* or Great Charter which made the crown answerable to the law.
John died after bingeing on his favourite meal – peaches in cider.

<u>Poles</u>

John I Albert of Poland (1492-1501)
John Casimir II Vasa of Poland (1649-1668)
John III Sobieski (1674-1696)

Swedes

John I of Sweden (1216-1222)
John II of Sweden (1497-1501)
John III of Sweden (1568-1592)

Dane

John of Denmark (1481-1513)

Byzantine Emperors

The Byzantine Empire was the Greek-speaking empire of the Middle Ages, with Constantinople (now Istanbul, Turkey) as capital.

John I Tzimisces (ruled 969-976)
John II Comnenus (1118-1143)
John III Ducas Vatatzes (1222-1254)
John IV Lascaris (1258-1261)
John VI Cantacuzenus (1347-1354)
John V Palaeologus (restored, second rule 1379-1391)
John VII Palaeologus (Grandson of John V, initially ruled for six months in 1390 and ruled again from 1399 to 1402 as co-emperor when Manuel II was away seeking aid from the West against the Turks)
John VIII Palaeologus, (1425-1448)

Top Dog Johns

<u>British Prime Ministers</u>

John Stuart, the third Earl of Bute, served as Tory Prime Minister from 1762 to 1763.

John Russell, the first Earl Russell, known as Lord John Russell before 1861, served twice as a Whig PM, from July 1846 to February 1852, and from October 1865 to June 1866.

John Major left school at 16 in 1959, with just three 'O' levels: History, English language, and English literature. He was turned down for a bus conductor job (because his arithmetic was too poor according to some newspapers) so he took correspondence course 'O' levels in Maths, British Constitution and Economics.

In the 1950s his father's garden gnome business failed, and the family moved to Brixton in 1955. He watched his first debate in the House of Commons in 1956, and attributes his political ambitions to that event and a chance meeting with former Labour Prime Minister, Clement Attlee, in London's King's Road.

His first job was as a clerk with insurance firm Pratt & Sons in 1959. Bored, he quit for a time and helped with his father's garden ornament business with his brother, Terry Major-Ball.

After a spell of unemployment, he started working for the London Electricity Board (where his successor as PM Tony Blair also worked when young) in 1963, and took a correspondence course in banking. He became an executive at Standard Chartered Bank in May 1965 and rose quickly through the ranks. He was sent to Nigeria by the bank in 1967, and nearly died in a car crash there.

He became a Conservative MP in 1979 and succeeded Margaret Thatcher as PM in 1990. He won a notable general election victory over Labour's Neil Kinnock in 1992 when the Tories were widely expected to lose. His defeat to Tony Blair in 1997 was one of the worst losses by a major party.

Major's quiet retirement was shattered by fellow Tory Edwina Currie's revelation that they had shared a passionate, four-year affair.

American Presidents

John Adams (1735-1826) was the second President of the USA, holding the post from 1797 to 1801 after two terms as the first Vice President. His opinion on the deputy job was:

"My country has, in its wisdom, contrived for me the most insignificant office ever the invention of man contrived or his imagination conceived."

John Quincy Adams (1767-1848), President – the
sixth – from 1825 to 1829, was better known for
his accomplishments as Secretary of State and as a
Congressman for 17 years after leaving the White House.

John Tyler was the first Vice President to assume the
office of President after the death of his predecessor. He
was in office from 1841 to 1845 and his most notable
accomplishment was the annexation of Texas.

Republican lawyer **John Calvin Coolidge** (1872-1933),
better known as plain Calvin, was the 30th President of
the United States from 1923 to 1929. He was the first
President to deliver a political speech on radio and the
only one to have his face on a coin during his lifetime, a
commemorative half dollar, in 1926.

The notoriously quiet man became known as 'Silent Cal'.
When writer Dorothy Parker sat next to him at dinner, she
joked: "Mr Coolidge, I've made a bet against a fellow who
said it was impossible to get more than two words out of
you." He replied famously: "You lose."

It was Parker who, on learning that Coolidge had died,
remarked: "How can they tell?"
Coolidge once wrote: "The words of a President
have an enormous weight and ought not to be used
indiscriminately."

John F. Kennedy was President from 1961-1963 when he was assassinated, aged 46, in Dallas while travelling with his wife, Jacqueline, in a motorcade. His assassin, Lee Harvey Oswald, was shot dead, leading to countless conspiracy theories about the reasons for his murder.

———◆———

VERY STUPID JOHNS

In 2003, John Kincannon, a Californian lawyer, was skimming leaves from his swimming pool when he noticed a palm branch caught in nearby power lines. He tried to remove it with his aluminium pool skimmer. Although smart enough to be a highly paid attorney, he didn't realise his activity would result in death by electrocution.

But he would have been proud at his family's action to sue both the utility company and the pool suppliers for failure to disclose the danger of poking a metal rod into power lines.

<u>Ig Nobel Prize winners</u>

1995
Nutrition – Presented to **John Martinez** of J. Martinez & Company in Atlanta, for Luak Coffee, the world's most expensive coffee, made from beans ingested and excreted by the *luak*, a bobcat-like animal native to Indonesia.

2003

Literature – Presented to **John Trinkaus**, of the Zicklin School of Business, New York City, for collecting data and publishing more than 80 detailed academic reports about things that annoyed him.

These included the percentages of:

- Young people who wear baseball caps with the peak facing the rear rather than the front
- Pedestrians who wear sport shoes that are white rather than any other colour
- Swimmers who swim laps in the shallow end of a pool rather than the deep end
- Car drivers who almost, but not completely, come to a stop at one particular stop-sign
- Commuters who carry attaché cases
- Shoppers who exceed the number of items permitted in a supermarket's express checkout lane
- Students who dislike the taste of Brussels sprouts.

UNDISPUTED JOHNS

John Weissmuller, more commonly known as Johnny, of Tarzan movie fame, was one of the best swimmers in the world during the 1920s. He won five Olympic gold medals and set 67 world records.

He won every race he ever swam but is still remembered more for his film career and the famous Tarzan call he invented.

BRITAIN'S OLYMPIC GOLD MEDAL JOHNS

Athens 1896
John Boland, tennis singles and doubles

Paris 1900
John Rimmer, athletics 4,000m steeplechase
John Symes, cricket
John Jarvis, swimming 1,500m and 4,000m freestyle
John Derbyshire, water polo

London 1908
John Douglas, boxing (middleweight)
John Robinson, hockey
John Astor, rackets doubles
John Fenning, rowing (coxless pair)
John Somers-Smith, rowing (coxless four)
John Fleming, shooting (25-yard small bore rifle, moving target)
John Postans, (shooting, clay pigeons, team)
John Derbyshire, swimming (4x200m freestyle relay)
John Duke, tug of war

Antwerp 1920
John Ainsworth-Davis, athletics (4 x 400m relay)
John Bennett, hockey
John McBryan, hockey
John Wodehouse, polo
John Sewell, tug of war

Paris 1924
John Faunthorpe, shooting (100m running deer, double shots, team)
John O'Leary, shooting (100m running deer, double shots, team)

Amsterdam 1928
John Lander, rowing (coxless four)

Los Angeles 1932
John Badcock, rowing (coxless four)

Garmisch-Partenkirchen 1936
John Coward, ice hockey
John Davey, ice hockey
John Kilpatrick, ice hockey

London 1948
John Wilson, rowing (coxless pair)

Mexico 1968
John Braithwaite, shooting trap (125 targets)

Innsbruck 1976
John Curry, figure skating

FOOTBALL JOHNS

John Charlton (b. 1935) better known as Jack, is the elder brother of Bobby and a member of the England team that beat West Germany 4-2 in the 1966 World Cup Final at Wembley. The centre-half played 35 times for England between 1965 and 1970 and was on the losing side just twice.

He appeared in 629 league games for Leeds United, winning a League Championship, a Second Division Championship, the FA and League Cups, two Fairs Cups and many runners-up medals. He was Footballer of the Year in 1967.

Patriotic Jack surprised the football world when he became the successful and popular manager of the Republic of Ireland national side from 1986 to 1995. He was made an Honorary Irish Citizen and Freeman of the City of Dublin.

Jack was nephew to Newcastle centre-forward 'Wor' Jackie Milburn and his other uncles, Jack, George, Jim (all Leeds) and Stan (Chesterfield, Leicester) played professionally in the top two divisions.

But Jack's own football career almost didn't happen. He seemed destined to follow many north-easterners down the local pit, but didn't like it, so he resigned and applied to be a police cadet.

He was due to be interviewed by the police in 1950, aged just 15, but a Leeds scout asked him to go for a trial and he played against Newcastle's youth team rather than attend his interview.

Welshman **John Charles**, believed by many to be the best all-round footballer Britain has produced, was skilful at centre-forward or centre-half. Charles made his league debut for Leeds against Blackburn Rovers in 1949, playing in defence. Two seasons later he played several matches as a striker, scoring twice in the second match.

He scored 150 league goals in eight years for Leeds, including 42 in the 1953-54 season.

He was the first world-class British footballer to have a successful foreign career and remains a hero at Italian club Juventus, for whom he scored 93 goals in 155 league games.

He is still known as *Il Buono Gigante* (the Gentle Giant) and was never booked or sent off in his career.

Charles also played for Roma, Cardiff City, Hereford United and Merthyr Tydfil, scoring 348 goals in 710 professional appearances.

For Wales, he netted 15 times in 38 internationals.

It's difficult, more than 40 years later, to convey how highly he was rated in world football. In the eyes of many he was, for a time, the finest player in the world.

John Haynes, commonly known as Johnny, was Britain's first £100 a week footballer and played for England 56 times between 1954 and 1962, scoring 18 goals and captaining the side in his last 22 appearances.

He was a unique talent with unmatched passing skills and a rare ability to dominate a game from the middle of the pitch when most top players were wingers such as Stanley Matthews and Tom Finney.

The gifted midfielder spent two decades without a trophy for unfashionable Fulham and his career was ended prematurely in 1969 by injuries in a car crash. He died in 2005, aged 71.

John 'Jock' Stein managed Celtic in 1967 when they were the first British club to win the European Cup, overcoming Inter Milan 2-1 in the final. The 'Lions of Lisbon' were unique among European champions in that all players had been born within 30 miles of their team's city, in this case Glasgow.

He led Celtic to a second European Cup Final in 1970 when they lost 2-1 in extra time to Holland's Feyenoord. Stein survived a near-fatal car crash in 1975 and stepped down as manager in 1977 after winning 11 Scottish Premier League titles, 11 Scottish Cups and six Scottish League Cups.

He became national team manager in 1978 and in September 1985, died of a heart attack at the end of a World Cup qualification match against Wales at Ninian

Park, Cardiff. Stein was denied a knighthood because of a brawl in an Intercontinental Cup match with Argentina's Racing Club in which four Celtic players were sent off.

Jamaican-born **John Barnes** was 15 when he moved to Watford to play a key part in the club's reaching the First Division in 1982.

He shot to international fame with a wonder goal for England against Brazil in Rio's Maracana Stadium in 1984, beating five or six players in a run from the halfway line.

The midfielder won FA and League Cups with Liverpool, 79 England caps and both the players' and (twice) the writers' Footballer of the Year awards.

His career developed when racism was rife, and even some England fans refused to cheer him. He suffered disgraceful abuse when playing club football but his dignity, skill and professionalism were important factors in ridding this ugliness from the English game.

Barnes rapped in two classic Top 10 pop songs.

First, in the 1988 Liverpool FA Cup anthem, Anfield Rap, was the memorable verse:

"You two Scousers are always yapping
I'm gonna show you some serious rapping
I come from Jamaica, my name is John Barn-es
When I do my thing the crowd go bananas"

His lines in New Order's 1990 World Cup hit, World in Motion, were:

"You got to hold and give,
But do it at the right time,
You can be slow or fast,
But you must get to the line

They'll always hit you, and hurt you,
Defend and attack,
There's only one way to beat them,
Get round the back

Catch me if you can,
Cos I'm the England Man
And what you're looking at,
Is the master plan

We ain't no hooligans,
This ain't a football song.
Three lions on my chest,
I know we can't go wrong."

John Trollope MBE (b. 1944) served Swindon Town for more than 40 years as player, coach and manager. His record for the number of league appearances for one club – 770 games between 1960 and 1980 – is unlikely to be matched. Trollope was an ever-present in the side for eight seasons from 1962, a run of 368 matches ending in August 1968 with a broken arm at Hartlepool United.

The injury meant he nearly missed Division Three
Swindon's greatest achievement but he recovered in time to
play in the 3-1 extra-time victory over top flight Arsenal at
Wembley in the 1969 League Cup Final.

John Terry (b. 1980) has already experienced more of
football's ups and downs than most, despite being still in
his twenties. Despite scoring winning FA Cup goals for
Chelsea in the quarter- and semi-finals of the 2001/02
season, he was left out of England's World Cup squad
after breaking a club curfew and being arrested outside a
nightclub.

He fought back to become Chelsea and England captain,
lifting two Premiership titles, in 2004 and 2005.

In 2007, he was the first skipper to lift the FA Cup at
the new Wembley Stadium after Chelsea's 1-0 win
over Manchester United. He also scored the first full
international goal at the new ground in England's 1-1 draw
with Brazil.

But in 2008 an injured Terry saw England fail to qualify for
the Euro 08 championships. And Chelsea narrowly missed
out on three trophies – including the European Champions
League where in the Moscow final Terry missed the penalty
shoot-out kick that would have won his club the trophy for
the first time.

John Madejski OBE, born Robert John Hurst in 1941, became chairman of Football League club Reading in 1990, rescuing the Royals from the receivers and a lowly position in Division 3. He built the £25 million Madejski Stadium and, in 2006, led the club to the top flight of English football for the first time.

The club was relegated in 2008 and Madejski says he is willing to sell the club to anyone who could take it forward to bigger and better things.

"I'll listen to sensible offers but from billionaires only," he said. "Millionaires need not apply."

John Portsmouth Football Club Westwood is one of the best known football fans in Britain. He changed his name in 1994 by deed poll and his appearance of blue and white dreadlocks, tattoos and blue and white outfits means he always catches the TV cameras' attention.

He's popular with most Portsmouth fans but his constant chiming of a bell to mark the Pompey Chimes has led to complaints from some.

Wembley Stadium refused to allow him to take any instruments to the 2008 FA Cup Final but he was consoled by his team's 1-0 win over Cardiff City. By day he puts on a suit and tie to run the family business, a second-hand bookshop in Petersfield.

ONE CAP WONDERS

<u>England</u>

John Clegg, The Wednesday, 1872
John Owen, Sheffield, 1874
John Bain, Oxford University, 1877
John Sands, Nottingham Forest, 1880
John Hudson, The Wednesday, 1883
John Leighton, Nottingham Forest, 1886
John Yates, Burnley, 1889
John Barton, Blackburn Rovers, 1890
John Cox, Derby County, 1892
John Pearson, Crewe Alexandra, 1892
John Veitch, Old Westminsters, 1894
John Hillman, Burnley, 1899
John Plant, Bury, 1900
John Calvey, Nottingham Forest, 1902
John Coleman, Woolwich Arsenal, 1907
John Bagshaw, Derby County, 1919
John Mew, Manchester United, 1920
John Bamber, Liverpool, 1921
John Fort, Millwall, 1921
John Davison, The Wednesday, 1922
John Alderson, Crystal Palace, 1923
John Butler, Arsenal, 1924
John Ball, Bury, 1927
John Pickering, Sheffield United, 1933
John Arnold, Fulham, 1933
John Bestall, Grimsby Town, 1935
John Crayston, Arsenal, 1937
John Morton, West Ham United, 1937

John Wright, Newcastle United, 1938
John Haines, West Bromwich Albion, 1948
John Lee, Derby County, 1950
John Wheeler, Bolton Wanderers, 1954
John Fantham, Sheffield Wednesday, 1961
John Angus, Burnley, 1961
Johnny 'John' Hollins, Chelsea, 1967
John 'Jimmy' Rimmer, Arsenal, 1976
John Richards, Wolverhampton Wanderers, 1973
John Gidman, Aston Villa, 1977

Scotland

John Blackburn, Royal Engineers, 1873
John Campbell, Celtic, 1880
John Goudie, Abercorn, 1884
John Graham, Annbank, 1884
John Inglis, Kilmarnock Athletic, 1884
John Gow, Queen's Park, 1885
John Cameron, Rangers, 1886
John McDonald, Edinburgh University, 1886
John Gow, Rangers, 1888
John Buchanan, Cambuslang, 1889
John Murray, Vale of Leven, 1890
John Hepburn, Alloa Athletic, 1891
John McCorkindale, Partick Thistle, 1891
John Johnstone, Kilmarnock, 1894
John Divers, Celtic, 1895
John Fyfe, Hearts, 1895
John Murray, Renton, 1895
John Cameron, Everton, 1896
John Gillespie, Queen's Park, 1896

John Kennedy, Hibernian, 1897
John Ritchie, Queen's Park, 1897
John Cross, Third Lanark, 1903
John 'Jack' Fraser, Dundee, 1903
John Lyall, Sheffield Wednesday, 1905
John Browning, Celtic, 1914
John Paterson, Leicester City, 1920
John Graham, Arsenal, 1921
John Gilchrist, Celtic, 1922
John McNab, Liverpool, 1923
John McKay, Blackburn Rovers, 1924
John Smith, Ayr United, 1924
John McDougall, Airdrieonians, 1926
John Gilmour, Dundee, 1930
John Murdoch, Motherwell, 1931
John Thomson, Everton, 1932
John Blair, Motherwell, 1933
John Brown, Clyde, 1938
John Divers, Celtic, 1938
John Anderson, Leicester, 1954
Johnny Dick, West Ham United, 1959
John Martis, Motherwell, 1960
John Plenderleith, Manchester City, 1960
John Sinclair, Leicester City, 1966
Johnny Doyle, Ayr United, 1975

SPORTING JOHNS

Sir John Berry Hobbs, known as **Jack Hobbs**, 'The Master' of Surrey and England, scored more runs (61,760) and more centuries (197) in first class cricket than any other player in the history of the game. He was the only England player and the only opening batsman to be named as one of the five Wisden Cricketers of the 20th century.

More than half of his centuries were scored after he had turned 40, and in 1929, aged 46, he was the oldest man to score a century in a Test match with 142 against Australia in Melbourne.

American 200 metre bronze medallist **John Carlos** (b. 1945) made the famous Black Power salute during a medal ceremony at the 1968 Mexico Olympics, alongside team-mate and gold medal winner Tommy Smith.

The men raised their left arms with hands in black gloves in a protest against USA civil rights abuses in what was voted the sixth most memorable TV event of the 20th century in one American survey.

After leaving athletics, Carlos had a short gridiron career in the National Football League and now works as a track and field coach for Palm Springs High School in California.

Although **John Peter Rhys Williams** (b. 1949), famously known as JPR, was one of Wales' best rugby union players,

his favourite sport was tennis. He won Junior Wimbledon in
1966 but pursued medical studies and played rugby union,
then an amateur sport.

He was one of the game's few great all-rounders and
helped Wales to six Triple Crowns and three Grand Slams,
captaining the side in 1979. As a British Lion he played in
series wins over South Africa and New Zealand. JPR loved
the game so much that he continued playing at a lower
level, for Tondu's third team, well into his 40s.

John Pulman was an English professional snooker player
who just missed out on the riches generated by the sport's
booming popularity due to colour TV. He was world
champion every year from 1964 to 1968 but when the 1969
championship became a knockout tournament he was
unable to defend his title successfully.

He lost to Ray Reardon in the 1970 final and went on to
become a commentator for ITV.

American tennis star **John McEnroe** (b. 1959) is famed
for his short temper and colourful language despite being
one of the sport's finest ever players. He won three singles
titles at the All-England Lawn Tennis Championships,
Wimbledon, in 1981, 1983, and 1984 and four US Open
singles titles between 1979 and 1984.

McEnroe seemed to thrive on conflict with officials and was
the only Wimbledon singles champion not to be granted

honorary membership after his first win. His "You cannot be serious" tirade at a Wimbledon umpire is now his catchphrase on the Masters circuit and was the title of his autobiography.

His comment to one official that "You are the pits of the world", was featured in The Pretenders' song, Pack It Up.

He is now a popular TV commentator and coaches young players.

Derbyshire-born **John Lowe** (b. 1945) won the darts world championship in three different decades, in 1979, 1987 and 1993, and was considered the gentleman of the game. He was the first to achieve the ultimate score, a nine-dart finish, on TV, during the 1984 World Matchplay tournament.

He won £102,000 for the achievement and went on to win the event.

Lowe also won two World Masters titles, two British Open titles and two British Matchplay championships, two World Cup Singles and three European Cup Singles Titles. He played for England more than 100 times and the England team were unbeaten during his seven-year run as captain.

He was the first high-profile darts player to look after his health and one of the few without a nickname until someone called him Old Stoneface, the title of his 2005 autobiography. He played in the televised stages of the world championships for a record 27 successive years and has tried but failed to qualify in 2006, 2007 and 2008.

Britain's **John Surtees** is the only racer to be world champion on two and four wheels. As a member of the Norton works motorcycle team he rode to victory in 68 of 76 races. He raced 350cc and 500cc bikes for the Italian MV Agusta team, winning seven world championships from 1956 to 1960.

Enzo Ferrari hired Surtees as his number one Formula 1 driver in 1963, and the following year he won the world championship. He went on to win three more Grand Prix races but no titles.

In 1995, Surtees had a row with team manager Eugenio Dragoni and never drove for Ferrari again. Surtees and Enzo Ferrari later agreed the split had been a "disastrous mistake" for both parties.

Soapy Johns

Coronation Street Character Johns

Love rat **John Stape**, played by Graeme Hawley, returned
to the Street in 2008 with a dramatic storyline. Cabbie
Stape kidnapped 17-year-old Rosie Webster, locking her in
an attic for weeks. He blamed the schoolgirl for destroying
his life after she seduced him and lost him his job as a
teacher.

Teachers' unions complained about Hawley's 'negative'
portrayal of their profession while angry shoppers,
confusing TV with reality, chased the actor and threw
frozen peas at him in a supermarket.

John Carter, played by Martin Gresham in 2001.
A medical company representative who went on a date
with Molly Hardcastle, only to be interrupted by a semi-
naked Kevin Webster wandering around the flat they
shared.

John Dalton, played by Andrew Frame in 1998.
He was a health and safety inspector who investigated Rita
Sullivan's gas fire when she was admitted to hospital with
carbon monoxide poisoning.

John Hargreaves, played by John Middleton in 1993.
Driver of the car that killed Lisa Duckworth in an accident.

John Harris QC, played by Terence Harvey in 2000. The barrister who represented Jim McDonald at his sentencing for Jez Quigley's murder.

John Spencer, played by Jonathan Barber in 1981. A 13-year-old boy fostered by Rita and Len Fairclough when his mum was in hospital.

John Wilding, played by John Bowler in 2002 was a scrap and plant-hire businessman whose wife Hazel had an affair with Streetcars' owner Vikram Desai.

Coronation Street Actors

Johnny Briggs played Cockney businessman Mike Baldwin in 359 episodes. One of his most popular story-lines was a romance with Ken Barlow's wife Deirdre. Rita Sullivan, played by Barbara Knox, appeared in Briggs' first scene in 1976 and in his final one 30 years later.

His character (who had suffered from Alzheimer's disease) collapsed and died in the street after a heart attack. He received a Lifetime Achievement Award in 2006 at the British Soap Awards and the MBE in the 2007 Queen's New Years Honours List.

Since leaving the Street, he has worked on _Miss Marple_ and _Holby City_, and become a regular in _Echo Beach_.
John Savident (b. 1938) played Fred Elliott from 1994

to 2008. Fred was scammed by Stacey who pretended to be an immigrant called Orchid, looking for a 'mail order' husband, but was really after his money.

Fred was turned down by Rita Sullivan, Audrey Roberts and Doreen Heavy, and finally fell in love with Shelley Unwin's mother, Bev.

More than 11 million viewers tuned in for his nuptials, only to see him die of a heart attack on his wedding day – after Audrey revealed she still loved him.

In 2000, actor Savident narrowly survived a knife attack at his home. A man was jailed for seven years after being found guilty of grievous bodily harm and robbery.

John Basham played brewery Newton & Ridley's yuppie executive Nigel Ridley in 1989 and 1990. Nigel wanted to turn The Rovers Return into an American theme-bar but publicans Bet and Alec Gilroy barricaded themselves in the pub until Cecil Newton killed the plan. Nigel later had an affair with Rovers barmaid Tina Fowler.

John Bowe played Duggie 'Crusher' Ferguson, an ex-rugby league player turned businessman, from 1999 to 2002. He came to Coronation Street after tracking down his son Tom, who blamed his dad for his mum's death and left the Street.

When the Boozy chain tried to convert The Rovers into the Boozy Newt, Duggie persuaded Fred Elliott and Mike Baldwin to invest in the pub with him. He later talked them into selling their shares cheaply to a "mystery owner" – who just happened to be Duggie himself.

Duggie's death came after he leaned over a banister which collapsed and he fell two floors. (Duggie had done a cowboy job of refurbishing the house.)

Other Corrie Actor Johns

John Barrett, played Monty Shawcross in 1990
John Batty, Cliff Humphries, 1976
John Bowler, John Wilding, 2002
John Branwell, Ed Malone, 1996
John Burton, DC Cody, 1997
John Challis, DS Phillips, 1977
John Collin, Paul Stringer, 1979
John Cording, chairman of magistrates, 1996
John Graham Davies, police sergeant, 2000
John Donnelly, Joe Harris and Dobber Dobson, both 1998
John Duttine, Alec Baker, 1977
John Elkington, Chris Melton, 2002
John Elmes, Leo Firman, 1995
John Finn, DS Rearden, 2001
John Griffin, DC Simon Cavanagh, 2000
John Gully, hospital clerk, 1998
John Henshaw, Mick Murphy, 1996
John Higgins, Sergeant Stevens, 1970
John Horsley, Rev Nuttall, 1983

John Jardine, Mr. Lewis, 1977; Tony Watkins, 1980; Gazette photographer, 1982; and Randolf Taylor 1990-1992

John Judd, Dr Cannon, 1977; and Sammy Chadwick, 1982

John Junkin, Bill Fielding, 1981

John Kirk, James Wright, 1998

John Labonowski, Frank Miller, 1982

John F Landry, Clifford Willis, 1976

John Langford, Mr. Stott, 1997

Johnny Leeze, (real name John Glen), Mr. Slater, 1982; and Harry Clayton, 1985

John McGregor, Dr Brooks, 1976

John McNulty, leading sea cadet, 1972

John Malcolm, Frank Pritchard, 1981

John Mirrlees, boy fishing by side of canal, 1976; and boy collecting money for the guy, 1977

John Normington, Mr. Groves, 1997

John O'Neill, Luke Ashton, 2001-2002

John Owens, Mr. Irwin, 1977

John Pickles, DI Conroy, 1976; PC Handley, 1978; and Arthur Watts, 1995

John Proctor, taxi driver, 1976; and Felix the barman, 1977

John Quayle, Capt. Platt, 1964; and Anthony Stephens, 2000-2001

John Rolls, jewellery shop assistant, 1976

John St Ryan, Charlie Whelan, 1993-1994

John Salthouse, Simon Lodge, 1976

John Sharp, Les Clegg, 1968

John Southworth, Mr. Conway, 1977

John Stratten, Arthur Crabtree, 1971

John Tordoff, Norman Hill, 1978; and Keith Hesketh, 1999
John Wheatley, Gary Hankin, 1977; and Joe Broughton, 1993-1994
John White, Bob Atkinson, 1980
John Who, rugby player, 1977

Writing Corrie

John Finch is one of only two people (along with H. V. Kershaw) who has served as writer, script editor and producer on Coronation Street.

His first script was screened in 1961, and he went on to pen 134 more until his last episode in 1970. He also created, edited and wrote the series *A Family At War* for ITV, followed by *Sam*, which won Broadcasting Press Guild and Writers Guild Awards.

EastEnders Character Johns

John Charrington, played by Jeremy Gittins in 2000.
Ian Beale's accountant. Ian ignored his advice which led to the collapse of his business empire.

John Davis, played by Huw Higginson in 2001.
The sleazy landlord doubled Laura's rent and then offered to help her in return for close personal favours.

John Fisher, played by David Hale, 1986.
Drag artiste hired by Angie Watts to perform at the Queen
Vic where he picked a fight with Ian Beale.

John Royle, played by Paddy Royce, 1990-1991.
Irish father of Eddie Royle, occasionally seen in the Queen Vic.

John Sparks, played by Richard Waters, 2002.
Turned down the chance of managing the Queen Vic after
seeing customers harassing Janine.

John Valecue, played by Steve Weston, 1996 and 1998.
Hitman hired by Cindy Beale to kill husband Ian. He was
unsuccessful and later jailed for life after another attempted
hit. Annie Palmer threatened to use her contacts to injure
him if he didn't implicate Cindy in the plot. John of course
did so, and Cindy was jailed for attempted murder.

John (no surname), played by William Halliday in 2001.
One of two men who picked up Zoe and Kat. John, old
enough to be Kat's dad, tried unsuccessfully to get her
drunk so he could have his wicked way.

John (no surname), played by Mark White in 2003.
Lisa Fowler's underworld contact who helped her to buy a
gun for the attempted murder of Phil Mitchell.

John (no surname), played by Ryan Cartwright in 1999. Raised money for the Bridge House halfway house.

EastEnders Actors

John Bardon (b. 1939) first appeared as Jim Branning in 1996. His career began in the 1960s and he appeared on classic programmes such as *Dad's Army*, *Only Fools and Horses*, *Casualty* and *Lovejoy*.

Film credits include *East is East*, *Fierce Creatures*, *Clockwise* and *One of Our Dinosaurs is Missing*. Among many stage appearances were parts in *Andy Capp*, *An Inspector Calls*, and *Kiss Me Kate*, for which he received an Olivier Award.

Bardon partnered with disco diva Jocelyn Brown in the BBC TV celebrity singing contest, *Just the Two of Us*, in 2007. The pair reached the semi-final as fellow *EastEnders* star Hannah Waterman went on to win with Marti Pellow.

John Partridge appeared in 2008 as Christian Clarke. He trained as a dancer at the Royal Ballet School and worked mainly in theatre before joining *EastEnders*. He has performed in many musicals, including *CATS*, *Tommy*, *Starlight Express*, *Grease* and *Miss Saigon*.

MINTED JOHNS

Norwegian tycoon **John Fredriksen** owns the world's biggest oil tanker fleet with more than 70 tankers and a wealth, estimated by *Forbes* magazine, to be £4 billion.

He made his fortune during the Iran-Iraq wars in the 1980s when his tankers picked up oil at great risk and huge profits. London-based Fredriksen rose up the *Sunday Times Rich List* from 66th wealthiest person in Britain in 2003, to eighth five years later.

John Caudwell (b. 1953) is an English billionaire who made his fortune in mobile phones. With his brother Brian, John started Midland Mobile Phones in 1987 and it took eight months to sell its first order of 26 phones.

By 2008, his Caudwell Group was selling 26 phones a minute. The group, including retailer Phones 4U, was sold to private equity firms for £1.46 billion in 2006. He spends much of his time on the Caudwell Children charity he founded for children in need, funding all overheads.

Mass-murdering Johns

The acid bath murderer, **John George Haigh**, began
his gruesome 'career' when he shot a young man, Donald
McSwann, in 1944. Haigh killed both of McSwann's
parents when they came to his workplace in London's
Gloucester Road looking for their son.

He established an efficient killing process, starting with the
isolation of the victim and an invitation to his 'workshop'.
The next stage was to shoot his prey with a .38 Webley
revolver. He then robbed the dead of cash and items he
could sell.

Finally, he disposed of the body using vats of industrial
acid but didn't realise that a corpse could not be completely
disposed of in acid. Some parts of the human body, such
as teeth and bone, and artificial items, including false teeth,
don't dissolve.

The media dubbed him the 'vampire of Kensington' after
he claimed to have drunk the blood of his victims.

But it was Haigh's false assumption that murder couldn't be
proved without a body which led to his downfall. Suspected
of killing 15 people, he was charged with just six murders:
William McSwann in 1944; Donald and Amy McSwann,
1945; Dr. Archibald Henderson, and his wife Rosalie, 1948;
and Mrs Olive Durand-Deacon, 1949.

When his two-day trial finished at Lewes Assizes in 1949,
the jury took 17 minutes to find him guilty. He was hanged

by the executioner Pierrepoint at Wandsworth Prison on August 10th 1949, aged 40.

John Christie (b. 1899) killed eight women in 13 years. His first victim was Ruth Fuerst, a tenant in Christie's flat above his home at 10 Rillington Place in London's Notting Hill. He went on to kill his own wife, a baby, prostitutes, tenants and various women he picked up.

His quiet and respectable manner seemed to have put him above suspicion and he was only discovered in 1953 when he moved house. The new owners noticed nasty smells under the floorboards – where they discovered a woman's legs.

His defence of not guilty due to insanity was rejected by an Old Bailey jury and he was hanged at Pentonville Prison, London, on July 15th 1953.

John Wayne Gacy sexually assaulted and killed 33 boys between 1976 and 1978 and was arrested when 27 bodies were found under his house. He had used his contracting business to attract young men eager for work.

Bizarrely, Gacy entertained local kids dressed as a clown. His father had been an abusive alcoholic who assaulted his wife and children. Gacy was executed by lethal injection, aged 52, in 1994.

His last meal comprised a dozen deep fried shrimp, a bucket of original recipe chicken from Kentucky Fried Chicken, a pound of fresh strawberries and French fries. Gacy had worked as a KFC manager in Iowa in the 1960s.

Former US Navy sailor **John Armstrong** was a quiet, 300-pound gentle giant, with boyish looks, who was respectably married with two children. But, Detroit police were suspicious when he reported seeing the body of a murdered prostitute in the Rouge River in 2000.

DNA tests linked him with the murder of another call-girl and he confessed to killing other sex workers and to 12 further murders around the world during his navy career from 1993 to 1998.

He went back on his confessions but received two life sentences plus 31 years for the murders of five Detroit prostitutes.

Australian **John Bunting** (b. 1966) is serving life for his leading role in the murder of 11 people in South Australia between 1992 and 1999. The crimes were uncovered when the remains of eight victims were found in barrels of acid in a rented former bank building in Snowtown, north of Adelaide.

Bunting was leader of a gang whose targets were people they knew. They cashed in their victims' welfare payments. When Bunting was young he burned insects in acid and became a Nazi. He claimed his killings were motivated by a deep hatred of paedophiles and homosexuals.

John E. Robinson (b. 1943) trawled the World Wide Web for kinky sexual partners under the name Slavemaster. But after the women had sex with him, they would disappear. He is thought to have killed eight victims between 1984 and 1999, and is currently on death row in a Kansas prison, fighting a 2003 sentence of death by lethal injection.

<hr>

TOP COP JOHNS

John Edgar Hoover was appointed director of the USA's Federal Bureau of Investigation (FBI) in 1924. His ruthless plan to make the bureau more professional included the firing of hundreds of agents.

Hoover also extended the FBI's activities to counter-intelligence and to the monitoring of political figures. It was said he had so much damaging information on the eight American presidents he served that none of them would ever sack him.

He was still in office when he died aged 77 in 1972.

Since his death, there have been lurid accounts that he had a secret life as a homosexual and/or a cross-dresser, but these claims have not been proven.

John Stalker (b. 1939) was a bobby on the beat who rose through the ranks to become Deputy Chief Constable of

Greater Manchester Police, the UK's biggest provincial force with more than 10,000 officers.

He chaired the Stalker Inquiry, a police investigation into shootings of suspected members of the Irish Republican Army by the Royal Ulster Constabulary, in 1983. His suspension from duty and removal from the inquiry in 1986, based on false allegations, caused a public outcry.

His book *Stalker* topped the best seller lists for many weeks with worldwide sales of more than 400,000. He is now a media personality, best known for appearing with his dog Drummer in TV ads for patio awnings.

━━◆◆◆◆━━

AUTHOR JOHNS

The 17th century Christian writer and preacher **John Bunyan** wrote much of his most famous work, *The Pilgrim's Progress*, during two periods of imprisonment for preaching without a licence.

The book is thought to be the most widely read in the English language and has been translated into more tongues than any book except the Bible. Bunyan wrote 60 books and tracts, of which *The Holy War* ranks next to *The Pilgrim's Progress* in popularity.

A passage from part two of *The Pilgrim's Progress* begins: "*Who would true Valour see*" and was used in the hymn *To Be a Pilgrim.*

John Steinbeck (1902-1968) was one of the 20th century's most celebrated authors, winning a Pulitzer Prize for his classic novel, *The Grapes of Wrath*, published in 1939, and the Nobel Prize for Literature in 1962. The Nobel judges cited "his realistic as well as imaginative writings, distinguished by a sympathetic humour and a keen social perception".

Steinbeck owed his glittering career to determination as much as skill. His first novel, *Cup of Gold* (1929) attracted little attention and his next two books, *The Pastures of Heaven* and *To a God Unknown*, were poorly received by critics, selling few copies. But his fourth novel, *Tortilla Flat* (1935), won a California literary award and launched his career.

Scotsman **John Buchan** wrote more than 100 books and enjoyed a long, successful career in journalism, publishing and government, but is remembered chiefly for one novel: *The Thirty-Nine Steps*, on which Sir Alfred Hitchcock made his celebrated film, *The 39 Steps*.

Buchan had been an administrator in South Africa after the Boer War, editor of *The Spectator* and war correspondent for *The Times*, MP for the Scottish Universities, a Director of Reuters, and Governor-General of Canada where he signed that country's entry into World War II, shortly before his death.

London-born **John Harvey** (b. 1938) is a prolific writer with more than 90 published books. He is best known as a writer of crime fiction, with the ten Charlie Resnick novels and numerous short stories his most popular works.

Harvey created the character as a believable policeman who investigated ordinary, everyday crime rooted in the drab lives of people in the city of Nottingham. He continues to work in radio drama where he has successfully adapted his own and others' work.

American novelist **John Irving,** born John Wallace Blunt, Jr. in 1942, is one of those rare writers whose fiction enjoys commercial success and critical acclaim. Since publishing his fourth novel, *The World According to Garp*, in 1978, he has written eight best-sellers, including *The Hotel New Hampshire* and *The Cider House Rules,* for which he won the 2000 Oscar for Best Adapted Screenplay.

Irving suffered from dyslexia before the illness had been recognised. Recurring themes in his work include New England, Iowa, prostitutes, bears, deadly accidents, a main character dealing with an absent or unknown parent, sexual relationships between young men and older women and other sexual relations.

The severing of body parts (such as tongues or fingers) appears in some novels.

He was also an accomplished wrestler and the sport features in many of his writings.

John Fowles' most famous novel, *The French Lieutenant's Woman*, set in Victorian Lyme Regis, was admired for having two endings, making it difficult to adapt for the cinema until Harold Pinter thought of writing the screenplay as a film-within-a-film.

Fowles was an instant sensation when his first novel, *The Collector*, appeared in 1963. *The Magus* followed in 1965 as another success. He died in 2005 as one of Britain's most celebrated authors.

John Keel is a controversial, New York-based author, journalist and ufologist. He interviewed thousands of people and reviewed more than 2,000 books over four years before publishing *UFOs: Operation Trojan Horse* in 1970. The book concluded that many aspects of UFO reports, including humanoid encounters, paralleled certain ancient folklore and religious encounters.

Keel believes UFOs are not extraterrestrial but belong to non-human intelligent beings on Earth. His 1976 book *The Mothman Prophecies*, an account of his investigation into sightings of a strange winged creature reported in West Virginia, was adapted into a 2002 movie starring Richard Gere and Alan Bates, each playing a separate part of Keel's personality.

Englishman **John Creasey** (1908-1973) was one of the most prolific writers of all time, publishing 600 books under his own name and more than 20 pseudonyms. He created many characters who appeared in a series of novels, the most famous being Gideon of Scotland Yard, on which the *Gideon's Way* TV series was based.

Other creations include *Department Z, Dr. Palfrey, The Toff, Inspector Roger West*, and *The Baron* (also made into a TV series). Incredibly, given his literary output, he found time to stand for election to Parliament, once as a Liberal and four times for his All Party Alliance which proposed to form a government of the best politicians from all parties.

Novelist, playwright and poet **J. B. Priestley** (1894-1984) was born John Boynton Priestley in 1894. He's best known for his plays, such as *An Inspector Calls* and for his best-selling novels, most notably *The Good Companions* and *Angel Pavement*. His huge output included essays, autobiography, social history, time theory and verse. Priestley also was active in politics as a founder member of the Campaign for Nuclear Disarmament in 1958.

Yorkshireman **John Braine** wrote 12 novels with his first, *Room at the Top* (1957), being turned into a successful film and forming the basis for a TV series *Man at the Top*.

English novelist and playwright **John Galsworthy** won the Nobel Prize in Literature in 1932. Among his many works were *The Forsyte Saga* and its sequels, *A Modern Comedy* and *End of the Chapter*. A 1967 TV adaptation of *The Forsyte Saga* brought his work to new generations of readers.

<hr>

PLAYWRIGHT JOHNS

English Jacobean dramatist **John Webster** was a contemporary of William Shakespeare, known for his tragedies, including *The White Devil* and *The Duchess of Malfi*, widely acclaimed as masterpieces of the early 17th century stage and still performed frequently. His violent and horrific drama turned off 18th and 19th century audiences but has found favour with today's theatre-goers.

John Dryden was an English poet, literary critic, translator and playwright, who so dominated the literary life of Restoration England in the 17th century that the period became known as the Age of Dryden. Unlike many dramatists of his age, Dryden wrote for the public and not for wealthy sponsors.

Among his so-called 'Restoration comedies' his best known was *Marriage A-la-Mode* (1672). In 1667, he published *Annus Mirabilis*, a lengthy poem describing 1666's English victory over the Dutch naval fleet and the Great Fire of London. The work established him as the pre-eminent poet of his generation, and led to his becoming Poet Laureate in 1668.

English poet and dramatist **John Gay** wrote *The Beggar's Opera* (1728), set to music by Johann Christoph Pepusch.

John Buckstone (1802-1879) was an English actor, playwright and comedian, who wrote 150 plays. He starred as a comic actor at the Adelphi Theatre and the Haymarket Theatre, and managed the Haymarket from 1853 to 1877. It was there in 1873 that Buckstone introduced theatre's first afternoon matinée performances, starting at 2pm.

John Osborne (1929-1994) was the original 'angry young man' who changed the face of British theatre. British plays were generally melodramas or middle class comedies until 1956, when Osborne's third work, *Look Back in Anger*, shocked audiences with its tale of rebellious Jimmy Porter's rage against post-war Britain.

The play, set in a shabby attic in a Midlands town, captured the feelings of many disillusioned British and set a trend for harsh, so-called 'kitchen-sink' dramas.

Laurence Olivier commissioned Osborne to write a play for him, and *The Entertainer*'s leading role, struggling comedian Archie Rice, is considered one of the greatest parts in 20th century drama. Osborne's output was a mixture of hits and misses, but he won a Best Screenplay Oscar in 1963 for his work on *Tom Jones*.

John Godber's observational comedy plays include *Up 'n' Under* (1980), featuring a bunch of losers in a northern pub's amateur rugby league team. Godber scripted and directed the film adaptation starring Griff Rhys Jones, Neil Morrissey and Samantha Janus.

His own favourite work is *Happy Families* (1991), an autobiographical play about growing up. Former teacher Godber also wrote for TV series *Brookside* and *Grange Hill*.

Sir John Mortimer (1923-2009) was an English barrister, dramatist and author whose best known character is Horace Rumpole, the claret-loving defence lawyer who first appeared in the 1975 BBC play *Rumpole of the Bailey*.

Rumpole, played by Leo McKern, became a regular feature in ITV schedules from 1978 to 1992 in the series of the same name. Mortimer has also published many novels featuring Rumpole.

He has written TV adaptations of Evelyn Waugh's novel *Brideshead Revisited* (1981), and of *Cider with Rosie* (1998) by Laurie Lee. His film screenplays included *Tea with Mussolini* (1999) directed by Franco Zeffirelli.

Scottish dramatist **John Byrne**'s stage plays include *The Slab Boys* and *Scotch and Wry* in the 1970s but he came to public attention in 1987 with *Tutti Frutti*, a TV comedy series about a Scottish rock band that helped to make the reputations of Emma Thompson, Robbie Coltrane and Richard Wilson.

Byrne has an even more successful career as an artist, with his first London one-man show taking place at London's Portal Gallery in 1967. He has designed jackets for Penguin Books and record covers for Donovan, The Beatles, Gerry Rafferty and Billy Connolly. It was Byrne who designed Connolly's famous giant banana boots.

Byrne has appeared in the gossip columns for his famously 'open' relationship with the actress Tilda Swinton. He doesn't read newspapers or watch TV.

POLITICAL JOHNS

Sir John Nott was Tory Defence Minister in March 1982 when Argentina invaded the Falkland Islands. Prime Minister Margaret Thatcher refused to accept his resignation over the national humiliation and he remained in the job until he left politics in 1985.

His autobiography was titled *Here Today, Gone Tomorrow*, a reference to when he walked out of a live TV interview with Sir Robin Day who had accused Nott of being a 'Here Today, Gone Tomorrow' politician. Storming out of TV studios was known as 'Doing a John Nott' for many years.

Nott's son, Julian, is a film composer, screenwriter and director, best known for the scores of the animated *Wallace & Gromit* films.

Labour's former Deputy Prime Minister **John Prescott** (b. 1938) is one of politics' most colourful characters. The former ship's steward and trade union activist was paraded as New Labour's link with the working class but always seemed to attract the wrong sort of publicity.

He gained the nickname 'Two Jags' for his extravagant lifestyle but always denied having a second Jaguar car and claimed his own Jag was second-hand. He once drove 200 yards in a convoy to deliver a speech on public transport at a Labour conference. He escaped legal action during the 2001 General Election after punching farmer Craig Evans who had thrown an egg at him.

Prescott confessed to an affair with his diary secretary Tracey Temple after the relationship was revealed in a national newspaper. And in his 2008 autobiography, *Prezza, My Story: Pulling no Punches*, he admitted his long-time struggle with the eating disorder *bulimia*.

Scotsman **John Reid** resigned his Cabinet post when Gordon Brown replaced Tony Blair as Labour Prime Minister. Reid was reported by the BBC as joking he might be offered the job of tea boy in a Brown government. He famously declared parts of the Home Office "not fit for purpose" when he became Home Secretary.

He was the first Roman Catholic to be Northern Ireland Secretary. As a heavy smoker, when he became Health Secretary, he tried to avoid a complete ban on public smoking with a plan for the law to cover only those pubs and restaurants serving food.

When Defence Minister, he sent 3,700 extra British troops to southern Afghanistan. He was appointed chairman of Celtic Football Club in 2007.

———◆———

CHILDREN'S TV PRESENTER JOHNS

A BBC Radio Bristol producer discovered farm manager **Johnny Morris** when he heard him telling amusing stories in a pub. Morris made his name with the charming narration of children's TV show *Tales of the Riverbank*, featuring real animals apparently operating miniature boats and cars.

He created the TV series *Animal Magic* in 1962, with himself as studio presenter and zookeeper. It was still popular when the BBC finished the series in 1983, judging its approach to be out of date.

Morris received an OBE in 1984 and was working on a new animal series called *Wild Thing* for Tyne Tees Television in 1999 when he collapsed and died, aged 82. He was buried with his old zookeeper's cap.

BBC TV chose **John Craven** (b. 1940) to anchor its first children's news programme in 1972 after first choice Jonathan Dimbleby turned it down. Craven wore a tie but not a suit and later presented in woolly jumpers.

John Craven's Newsround gave children background to headlines about adult issues and went into children's subjects such as school dinners, school uniform and pocket money. Craven became programme editor in 1986 and the title changed to *Newsround* the following year. Craven left the show in 1989 and received an OBE in 2000.

Actor **John Noakes**' (b. 1934) 12-and-a-half years on *Blue Peter* was the longest spell by any of the programme's presenters. He looked after *Blue Peter* dog Patch who was replaced by Border Collie Shep in 1971, resulting in the catchphrase "Get down, Shep" as he tried to control the energetic hound.

After Noakes left the programme in 1978, he and his wife set off to sail around the world but were shipwrecked in a hurricane. They tried again in 1984, stopped in Majorca and liked it so much that they stayed, and are still there.

Noakes initially refused to attend a show to mark *Blue Peter*'s 50th anniversary in 2008 because of a long-time disagreement with producer Biddy Baxter. But he changed his mind when the Queen made a personal request for him to take part.

Johnny Ball (b. 1938) has made science and maths entertaining to children in a number of TV series, including the BBC's *Think of a Number* and *Think Again,* and *Johnny Ball Reveals All* on ITV.

His TV shows and videos won 12 awards, including a BAFTA and a New York International Emmy nomination. Ball's daughter Zoe is a popular TV presenter and radio DJ.

Scotsman **John Leslie** is a former presenter of *Blue Peter*, ITV's *This Morning* and game show *Wheel of Fortune*. In 2003, he was cleared on two counts of indecent assault against an actress in 1997 and was told by the judge that he left the court "completely innocent and without a stain on my character".

In 2008, British media reported he had been arrested in relation to another offence. No charges were brought against him but he lost his job as *This Morning* presenter and abandoned his TV career. He became a property developer in his native Edinburgh but it was rumoured he was planning a TV comeback in 2009.

——————

What does John mean, exactly?

Many people think mistakenly that the toilet was invented by a Mr. Thomas Crapper in the 18th century. In fact, simple toilets have been used since Babylonian times and it was **John Harrington** in 1596 who invented an indoor water closet for Queen Elizabeth I.

Harrington published a book with tasteless puns about his own invention and the toilet dropped into obscurity for nearly 200 years. There was a Mr. Crapper around at the time who, conveniently, happened to be a plumber. The American word for toilet, 'John', is thought to derive from Harrington's invention.

BROADCASTER JOHNS

John Arlott's (1914-1991) Hampshire accent and deep love and knowledge of cricket made him a legendary commentator and one of the most recognisable voices of BBC Radio's long-running *Test Match Special*.

He covered every single home Test match from 1946 to 1980. At the end of his final commentary at Lord's, the crowd and the players of England and Australia stood and applauded.

The British public would have missed out on Arlott's gifts if he had not been discovered by accident in 1945 when he was a police sergeant in Southampton. His address on behalf of the police to King George VI was broadcast and BBC executives recognised a voice that was perfect for radio.

Born John Robert Parker Ravenscroft, **John Peel** was the longest-serving BBC Radio 1 DJ when he died aged 65 from a heart attack in 2004. His broadcasting career began unpromisingly in 1967 with a two-hour slot from midnight on pirate radio station Radio London. It was here that a secretary suggested he adopted the name John Peel (after the 19th century Cumberland huntsman).

When the station closed that year, Peel joined the new BBC Radio 1 where he became famous for championing new genres and bands. Artists who credited Peel for giving their careers a major boost included T-Rex, Led Zeppelin, Mike Oldfield, David Bowie, The Faces, The Sex Pistols, Pink

Floyd, The Clash, Buzzcocks, Joy Division, Def Leppard, Pulp, The Smiths and The White Stripes.

A famous Scouser, Peel wore Liverpool FC's red and white when he walked down the aisle to the club song You'll Never Walk Alone to marry Sheila Gilhooly in 1974. Their sheepdog, Woggle, was a bridesmaid.

John Stapleton worked on BBC TV's *Nationwide* from 1975 until 1980. He has also worked at TV-am as a reporter and as a presenter of *Good Morning Britain*. He fronted the consumer programme *Watchdog* with wife Lynn Faulds Wood, and the live morning talk show *The Time, The Place*.

He presented *ITV News* several times and is a contributor to the BBC series *Grumpy Old Men*. In 2008 he revealed on BBC's *The One Show* that he had suffered from the eating disorder *anorexia nervosa* for many years in his youth.

John Suchet (b. 1944) was one of the UK's best known television newsreaders and reporters, working for ITN for 32 years until 2004, and for Channel Five in 2006. He was Television Journalist of the Year in 1986 and Television Newscaster of the Year in 1996. His other passion is classical music, and in the late 1990s he published *The Last Master,* a widely acclaimed trilogy on the life and work of Beethoven.

John Humphrys (b. 1943) is the longest-serving presenter of BBC Radio 4's early morning *Today* programme with a reputation as a tough interviewer. Many politicians have criticised his technique, with Jonathan Aitken famously accusing him of "poisoning the well of democratic debate".

He began his journalism career as a 15-year-old cub reporter on the *Penarth Times* and at 28 was the BBC's first full-time TV correspondent in the United States and the youngest television foreign correspondent. He has picked up many awards including Sony Golds for lifetime achievement and journalist of the year.

He covered Watergate and the resignation of President Nixon. Today, he presents *On the Ropes* on Radio 4 and *Mastermind* on BBC TV.

John McCririck (b. 1940) is an eccentric TV horse racing pundit, instantly recognisable by his deerstalker hat, tweed coat and large sideburns, as well as his use of the traditional tic-tac signals. He's a famous male chauvinist who delights in making comments that outrage popular opinion.

He reached a wider audience in 2005 when he was a sulky contestant on *Celebrity Big Brother*. He refused to join in the show's tasks, walked around in giant white underpants and stayed silent for three days in protest at the lack of Diet Coke in the house.

He calls his wife Jenny "The Booby", and in 2006, the pair took part in *Wife Swap* with Edwina Currie and her husband (also called John). Currie objected to McCririck's habits, which included eating meals in bed and refusing to cook or drive the car.

The Euro 2008 final between Spain and Germany from Vienna was commentator **John Motson**'s (b. 1945) last major TV showpiece after more than 35 years as the BBC's voice of football.

'Motty' covered nine European Championships, nine World Cups and 34 FA Cup finals. He still commentates on *Match of the Day* and Radio 5 Live. His first TV commentary was the FA Cup replay between Hereford and Newcastle in 1972.

It was expected to be a five-minute segment but Hereford's shock 2-1 win, Ronnie Radford's famous 30-yard strike and a huge pitch invasion gave Motson a great career break.

His occasional mistakes only seemed to add to his appeal to the public with "for those of you watching in black and white, Spurs are in the all yellow strip" one of his finest.

He received an OBE in 2001 and was Sports Commentator of the Year in 2004.

Veteran political journalist **John Sergeant** (b. 1944) became a highly improbable celebrity when he appeared on the BBC's popular *Strictly Come Dancing* competition in 2008.

Viewers loved his humorous approach to the contest and continued to vote for him in big numbers, but the judges were aghast at his failure to take the programme seriously. Professional choreographer and judge, Arlene Phillips, said that instead of rehearsing Sergeant "sits and reads *The Guardian*".

As a national controversy raged as to whether Sergeant would be allowed to win with his populist approach, the man himself resigned, saying: "It was always my intention to have fun on the show and I was hoping to stay in as long as possible. The trouble is that there is now a real danger that I might win the competition. Even for me, that would be a joke too far."

TV presenter, voiceover and commentator **John Sachs** is best known for his narration on the original series of *Gladiators* and as a DJ on London's 95.8 Capital FM. He is the son of Andrew Sachs, who played Spanish waiter Manuel in *Fawlty Towers*.

Hero Johns

In 2008, two air pilot Johns became heroes when their skill and courage rescued two separate flights in peril.

In January, 41-year-old co-pilot **John Coward** admitted he thought everyone on Flight BA38 from Beijing was going to die in a "catastrophic disaster" when his 777's engines lost power at 600ft as it came to land at Heathrow Airport.

He said he acted "on instinct" to land the aircraft and save the lives of 152 passengers and crew. The modest hero told the media: "I was only doing my job."

In July, Qantas pilot **John Bartels** thanked his basic training for saving the lives of 365 people on board after an explosion tore a hole in his jumbo jet.

He said he automatically took the action needed to save flight QF30 and land the plane at Manila airport in the Philippines.

"As soon as we realised this was a decompression, I immediately pulled out my memory checklist," the Eltham-based pilot told the *Sunday Herald Sun*.

"I have no doubt that every Qantas captain in the same situation would have had the same result."

In 1986, **John McCarthy** (b. 1956) was on his first foreign assignment as a TV newsman in Beirut when he was grabbed from his car by Islamic terrorists and held hostage

for five years (1,943 days). He spent much of the time
chained to a radiator fearing death almost every day.

His former fiancée Jill Morrell set up 'The Friends of John
McCarthy' to keep his plight in the public eye, and the
British people sensed a happy ending to their romance
when McCarthy was released in 1991.

The pair wrote a book together, *Some Other Rainbow*, but
separated amicably in 1994 and McCarthy married Anna
Ottewill in 1999.

He formed a strong bond with Irish fellow hostage Brian
Keenan and an account of their ordeal was made into a
2004 film, *Blind Flight*. McCarthy works as a TV and radio
journalist and as a business speaker where he describes the
self-motivation and courage needed to stay alive and sane
and how to apply these to life and at work.

John Nichol flew RAF Tornadoes for 15 years and was shot
down by Iraqis on his first mission in the first Gulf War in
1991. He was paraded on worldwide TV with clear evidence
of torture on his face shocking viewers around the world.

He was tortured at Abu Ghraib prison where US troops
would later be accused of abusing detainees during the
second Gulf War.

He was released by the Iraqis at the end of the Gulf War
in 1991, returned to active duty policing an exclusion
zone as part of the United Nations force in Bosnia, and
left the RAF in 1996. He co-authored a book, *Tornado
Down*, with fellow pilot John Peters, about this Iraq

experience and is now a broadcaster and journalist on military affairs.

Glaswegian baggage handler **John Smeaton** became an international celebrity when he tackled suspected bombers at Glasgow Airport in June 2007.

He told *ITN News*: "Glasgow doesn't accept this. That's just Glasgow. We'll set about ye."

Smeaton, who also dragged a bystander away from a burning jeep, was presented with the Queen's Gallantry Medal by the Queen in 2008. A tribute website johnsmeaton.com called on people to "pledge a pint for Smeato" at the Glasgow Airport Holiday Inn, and more than 1,400 pints were bought for him within a few days.

In October 2008, Smeaton recovered after two weeks in a coma following a near-fatal asthma attack.

MISSING JOHNS

Prince John was born in 1905, on the Sandringham Estate, Norfolk, the youngest child of Prince George, the Prince of Wales and of Princess Mary, Princess of Wales.

His parents became King George V and Queen Mary, and John was sixth in line to the throne. But the boy suffered from epilepsy and autism, and the Royal Family sheltered him from public view.

John died aged 13 after a fit in the early hours of January 18th 1919. He has since been called "The Missing Prince".

Labour MP **John Stonehouse** (1925-1988) faked his own death in the manner of popular 1970s TV comedy character, Reginald Perrin, played by Leonard Rossiter. He placed a pile of clothes on a Miami beach in 1974 to fake his drowning, leaving behind a wife and a daughter.

He was arrested on Christmas Eve, five weeks after his disappearance, in Melbourne, Australia, where he had established a new identity and was living with his former secretary Sheila Buckley. The Australian police wrongly believed they had caught the missing British murder suspect Lord Lucan.

Stonehouse served three years of a seven-year jail term for theft, fraud and deception in a series of fraudulent businesses.

In March 2002, coastguard rescue teams called off the search for missing 51-year-old **John Darwin**, who was last seen taking to the sea in his canoe near Hartlepool. As his sons, Mark and Anthony, comforted their mother, Anne, the broken remains of Darwin's red canoe were found, apparently confirming he had drowned.

Mrs Darwin duly cashed in a life insurance policy.

Five years later, Darwin walked into a central London police station, claiming to have amnesia. But police later arrested him and in July 2008 he was jailed for six years and three months after pleading guilty to seven charges of obtaining cash by deception and a passport offence. His wife was jailed for three months longer on 15 convictions for fraud and money laundering.

Their trial revealed he had been living next door to the family home during his 'disappearance'. The judge told the couple the biggest victims of their fraud were their sons, who want no more contact with their parents.

———⋙◆⋘———

ASTRONAUT JOHNS

The 40-year-old **John Glenn** became an American hero in 1962 when he was the first of his countrymen to orbit the Earth. He travelled 81,000 miles (130,000 km) whilst circling the planet three times at more than 17,000 mph (27,000 kph).

As he re-entered the atmosphere after a four-hour and 56-minute journey Marine Lieutenant Glenn said: "Boy, that was a real fireball." His mission took place ten months and ten days after Soviet cosmonaut Yuri Gagarin had become the first man in space.

Among the tasks Glenn performed in orbit were the first experiments in eating food in weightless conditions. It turned out to be an easy but not very tasty experience.

John Blaha completed 361 combat missions in the Vietnam War before he joined NASA. He logged 161 days in space on five missions between 1989 and 1997. His journeys included the longest ever duration for a Space Shuttle flight of 14 days when he and his crew ran extensive medical experiments on themselves and 48 rats.

Blaha learned Russian for his final outing in September 1996 when he transferred to the Mir Space Station and spent four months with its Russian cosmonaut crew.

John Creighton completed three Space Shuttle missions between 1985 and 1991.

John Fabian's first Space Shuttle assignment in 1983 was the second flight of the *Challenger* and the first with a five-person crew. His second was in 1985.

John Herrington's only space assignment saw him perform three 'extra-vehicular activities' totalling 19 hours and 55 minutes in 2002. His spacecraft also brought home a crew from their six-month stay aboard the station.

Welshman **John Llewellyn** was poised to be the first British astronaut when he joined NASA as a scientist-astronaut in August 1967. He completed academic training and started pilot instruction in preparation for manned space flights.

Dr. Llewellyn withdrew from the programme in 1968 "for personal reasons" and went to work for the University of South Florida. The first Briton in space in 1991 was 27-year-old, Sheffield-born Helen Sharman who flew with the Soviet Soyuz TM-12 space crew.

John 'Mike' Lounge has logged over 482 hours in space on three Space Shuttle assignments. His second flight on *Discovery* in 1988 was the first to be flown after the *Challenger* disaster in which all seven crew members died.

Back-up astronaut **John Swigert** (1931-1982) knew only 72 hours before lift-off that he would be replacing Thomas Mattingly as Apollo 13 command module pilot. Programmed for ten days, the April 1970 mission would be the first landing in the hilly, upland *Fra Mauro* region of the moon.

But a failure of the service module's oxygen system, 55 hours into the flight, turned the lunar expedition into a drama that caught the imagination of the whole world as the crew fought for their lives. It was Swigert who reported: "Houston, we've had a problem here" which is often misquoted as "Houston, we have a problem".

Swigert, fellow crewmen James Lovell, spacecraft commander, and Fred Haise, lunar module pilot, worked with Houston ground controllers to convert the lunar module *Aquarius* into a lifeboat. Kevin Bacon played Swigert in Ron Howard's 1995 film, *Apollo 13*.

John Young (b. 1930) was NASA's most experienced astronaut whose career began with the first manned Gemini flight, Gemini 3, in 1965 and ended with the first Spacelab mission in 1981. He logged 835 hours of space time in six flights.

On Gemini 3, he operated the first computer on a manned spacecraft. He flew as commander on Gemini 10 in 1966 and was command module pilot of Apollo 10 three years later. With Apollo 16 he conducted experiments on the moon's surface as commander in 1972. He and Charlie Duke collected 200 lb (90kg) of rocks and drove 16 miles (25.7 km) in the lunar rover.

He commanded the first Space Shuttle flight in 1981, when the orbiter *Columbia* was the first manned spaceship tested during ascent, on orbit, and re-entry without the benefit of previous unmanned missions.

WHAT DOES JOHNNY MEAN, EXACTLY?

Johnny Foreigner tends to be used by xenophobic Brits to stereotype all people who are not, well, British. The phrase is usually loaded to suggest that Johnny Foreigner is either not to be trusted or cannot be expected to measure up to the Brits' own extremely high standards.

———≫◆≪———

PUTTING JOHNS

John Daly (b. 1966) is probably the most remarkable golfer ever to play on the professional tour. He arrived on the scene almost by accident in 1991 at the PGA Championship, one of golf's four majors, at Carmel, Indiana.

When Norman Price dropped out, Daly was in ninth position – as a standby player – to take his place but none of the eight men before him were able to play.

Daly shocked everyone with a first round score of 69, without even having a practice round. He won the tournament with scores of 69-67-69-71, beating Bruce Lietzke by three strokes. He won a few smaller competitions before stunning the golf world again in 1995 by winning another major, the (British) Open, in a play-off with Italian Costantino Rocca at St. Andrews.

In his autobiography, *John Daly: My Life In and Out of the Rough*, the golfer admitted to his drinking and gambling addictions, claiming to have run up gambling losses of $60 million.

The amazing story of LaVerne Moore, alias **John Montague** (1904-1972), is told in a book by Leigh Montville called *The Mysterious Montague: A True Tale of Hollywood, Golf, and Armed Robbery*. Montville said Montague was the greatest golfer who never won a tournament, mainly because he never entered one.

In 1930, Montague was one of four men who robbed a restaurant at gunpoint in upstate New York, and the only one who escaped arrest. He later became a darling of Hollywood, with Oliver Hardy, W. C. Fields, Johnny Weissmuller, Randolph Scott, Douglas Fairbanks, Mary Pickford, Howard Hughes and Bing Crosby among his friends.

Montague once beat Crosby at golf, playing with a rake instead of clubs. He could chip a ball across a room into a glass or knock a bird off a high wire with a shot. Police decided that Montague was in fact Moore, the fugitive wanted for armed robbery, but the public cheered when he was acquitted at his trial.

Anyone who finds golf difficult should imagine what it must be like to play with just one arm. Amateur golfer **John Roberts** does just that, playing back-handed with his left arm, as he was born without a right hand.

He started playing when 11 years old at Ormskirk Golf Club, Lancashire. At 29, he played off a nine handicap and was beaten in the final of the World One Arm Championships at Elie Golf House Club, near St. Andrews, in 1977. He gave up the sport the following year to concentrate on his family and business but picked up the clubs again in his 50s.

In 2008, the 59-year-old Roberts scored a 157-yard (144 metre) hole in one with a five iron from the 15th tee at Hurlston Hall Golf Club, near Ormskirk. It was his first ace. Roberts said: "It was a terrible round otherwise and I got taken to the cleaners in the bar afterwards."

Famous John Quotes

"No man is an island, entire of itself; every man is a piece of the continent."
John Donne, poet

"Men are motivated and empowered when they feel needed. Women are motivated and empowered when they feel cherished."
John Gray, author

"A thing of beauty is a joy forever."
John Keats, poet

"Mankind must put an end to war before war puts an end to mankind."
John F. Kennedy, US president

"In the long run we are all dead."
John Maynard Keynes, economist

"If everyone demanded peace instead of another television set, then there'd be peace."
John Lennon, musician

"In this life he laughs longest who laughs last."
John Masefield, poet and author

"Better to reign in hell than serve in heaven."
John Milton, poet

"Ideas are like rabbits. You get a couple, learn how to handle them, and pretty soon you have a dozen."
John Steinbeck, author

"Sex is like money; only too much is enough."
John Updike, writer

"Life is tough, but it's tougher when you're stupid."
John Wayne, actor

There is every chance we have missed a John, or two.

Let us know at **www.stripepublishing.co.uk**

ACKNOWLEDGEMENTS

Thank you and respect to all the Johns in history and contemporary life who have made this such an interesting book to research and write.

And thanks, too, to the friends and family, too many to name, for their suggestions of their favourite Johns.

Appreciation, too, to Dan Tester at Stripe Publishing, for his patience and advice.

And finally, best wishes to all the Johns on the planet: You make the world go round.

BIBLIOGRAPHY

John Lennon: The Life by Philip Norman; HarperCollins Entertainment; 1 Oct 2008

Encyclopaedia Britannica; Encyclopaedia Britannica (UK) Ltd; Jan 1st 1968

The Clash: Strummer, Jones, Simonon, Headon by The Clash; Atlantic Books; Oct 1st 2008

J. R. R. Tolkien: A Biography by Humphrey Carpenter; HarperCollins Publishers Ltd; New edition, Jan 2nd 2002

Up in the Clouds, Gentlemen Please by John Mills; Gollancz; 2nd revised edition, Oct 4th 2001

Searching for John Ford by Joseph McBride; Faber and Faber; New edition, Jul 1st 2004

The Pythons' Autobiography by The Pythons by Graham Chapman, John Cleese, Terry Gilliam, Eric Idle, Terry Jones, Michael Palin and Bob McCabe; Orion, New edition, Sep 15th 2005

Britain's Prime Ministers by G. R. R. Treasure and Roger Ellis; Shepheard-Walwyn (Publishers) Ltd; Nov 1st 2005

The Complete Book of U.S. Presidents: from George Washington to George W. Bush by William DeGregorio; Barricade Books Inc., USA; 5th revised edition, Jun 2nd 2004

The Serial Killer Files: The Who, What, Where, How, and Why of the World's Most Terrifying Murderers by Harold Schechter; Ballantine Books; Dec 2003

Recommended Websites

www.absoluteastronomy.com/topics/Superstars
www.afterquotes.com
www.allwords.com
www.anorak.co.uk
www.answers.com
www.askmarsvenus.com
www.askoxford.com
www.bbc.co.uk
www.screenonline.org.uk
www.biography.com
www.bloomsbury.com
www.britisholympians.com
www.britishtheatreguide.info
www.buzzle.com
www.dictionary.cambridge.org
www.championships.wimbledon.org
www.city-of-bradford.com
www.1911encyclopedia.org
www.cmmol.net
www.corrie.net
www.cricinfo.com
www.cricketarchive.com
www.dailymail.co.uk
www.dark-horse.co.uk
www.digitalspy.co.uk
www.doweb.co.uk
www.doollee.com
www.ecoresearch.net
www.encarta.co.uk
www.englandcaps.co.uk

www.englandfootballonline.com
www.ewtn.com
www.filmsite.org
www.fao.org
www.forbes.com
www.formula1.com
www.fortunecity.com
www.thefreedictionary.com
www.golfersmagazine.co.uk
www.guardian.co.uk
www.highbeam.com
www.historylearningsite.co.uk
www.horrorstew.com
www.huffingtonpost.com
www.imagi-nation.com
www.independent.co.uk
www.indymedia.org.uk
www.olympic.org
www.imdb.com
www.jbpriestley.co.uk
www.jla.co.uk
www.johndaly.com
www.jgrisham.com
www.johnlewis.com
www.johnmccarthytalks.co.uk
www.johntitor.com
www.legendsofdarts.com
www.mayhem.net
www.mirror.co.uk
www.history.nasa.gov
www.nationmaster.com
www.nyt.co.uk

www.onelook.com
www.peevish.co.uk
www.phrases.org.uk
www.rampantscotland.com
www.rbkc.gov.uk
www.salon.com
www.scotlandsupportersclub.com
www.scottishfa.co.uk
www.soccerbase.com
www.news.sky.com
www.ssje.org
www.eastenders.soyouthink.com
www.telegraph.co.uk
www.time.com
www.timesonline.co.uk
www.trutv.com
www.tvlives.com
www.tvpresenters.co.uk
www.ukpol.co.uk
www.uktv.co.uk
www.brad.ac.uk
www.usatoday.com
www.walfordweb.co.uk
www.whitehouse.gov
www.worldwidewords.org
www.100welshheroes.com
www.1001cocktails.com